Lucie's Hope:

George Levy Mueller's Memoirs of the Holocaust

By
George Levy Mueller
with
Roslyn Z. Weedman

ISBN 978-0-7414-1449-6

INFINITY PUBLISHING
1094 New DeHaven Street, Suite 100
West Conshohocken, PA 19428-2713
Toll-free (877) BUY BOOK
Local Phone (610) 941-9999
Fax (610) 941-9959
Info@buybooksontheweb.com
www.buybooksontheweb.com

In memory of my parents, Max and Lucie Hope Levy, who did not survive the Holocaust.

To my wife and children who supported me in the writing of this book.

To my fifteen grandchildren.

And to my Uncle Joseph and Aunt Irmgard who brought my sister Ursula and me to America.

-- George Levy Mueller

In memory of my father, Rod Weedman, a USMC veteran of World War II.

To my son, James, who is the undisputed master story teller in the family.

To my daughter, Cris, whose life and efforts are an inspiration.

And most especially to my husband, Marty, whose love, courage, humor, patience, and steadfastness sustain me.

-- Roz Weedman

Special thanks to Delta College for the sabbatical that made this book possible and to my friends at Delta College, especially the Barnes & Noble Saturday morning Girlfriends, Nadine Nader for her reading and sharing of resources, and Larry Levy for his reading, resources, and support, and all my colleagues who provided encouragement in countless ways.

Preface

By Roz Weedman

Helping George Levy Mueller make a record of his Holocaust experiences turned out to be more than a simple recollection of past events, however horrific or, sometimes, uplifting. Rather, this project emphasized the truth that history isn't absolute but unfolds and comes back to us with the process of discovery and recovery.

Holocaust survivors are particularly challenged to do more than remember, having commonly let decades go by without articulating their histories. They must also pull together their pasts from the various available fragmented sources. George has a lot going for him in this process. He's got, of course, his memories. But he also has childhood photographs that survived the Holocaust, his sister Ursula to talk to, his cousin Margaret, and his own ability to locate information and documents that put specific detail to some of George's childhood recollections. Additionally, he has some surviving friends from his youth with whom he maintains contact who add important elements.

The unfolding drama of discovery as to what, exactly, happened to George's mother, Lucie Hope Levy, has been one of the surprises of putting this story together. Although her death during the Holocaust was certain, the facts surrounding her final months and place of death were not discovered until near the end of this project. In many respects, her presence encircles George's story from the beginning to the end.

A comment on the style of the narrative: All of the story that takes place in the 1930's and 1940's is in George's first person voice. I have enjoyed his wonderful, intelligent, straight-forward voice, and everyone involved in this project understands how important it is that George's distinctive voice be clearly heard by the reader. The parts of George's story that are set in the year 2000, I've written in the first person in order to bring in observations and events critical to George's life. But, I want to emphasize, even though the narrator changes depending on whether we are in the past or closer to the present, all of this is George's story, no one else's, and all of it is relevant to his Holocaust past. I've had the privilege of observation. His wife, Katie, and his five children have brought their perspectives into this book also. Each of these contributions serves to let us know more about George's life.

George is adamant that the events of the Holocaust as he knows them carry sufficient authority so that he personally eschews additional moralizing. As he put it one day, the implications of this story are either very clear from its telling or, for those who don't understand the lessons, no amount of moralizing will make them wiser.

With these notes on the text out of the way, then, I believe no one can introduce George better than his wife, Katie.

Introduction

By Katie Mueller

When George and I met in college in the early 1950's, he told me vague stories about his background. His parents, he said, were killed while working for the Dutch underground. He told stories about their heroic feats and his happy Dutch childhood in Eersel.

But after we became engaged, he approached me, physically trembling, his voice shaking, and blurted out, "I'm Jewish. My parents were killed by the Nazis. I spent two years in a concentration camp." I felt his anguish and also felt terrible about his history with the Nazis, but the part about being Jewish didn't mean much to me at the time.

George was a Catholic, like me, a graduate of a Catholic high school and college; all his friends were from these schools; he had been taught by nuns, brothers, and priests. He was even an altar boy and could translate from the Latin prayer books. To an Irish Catholic girl, those things were familiar and counted in finding a partner for life.

During the early years of our marriage, we were busy making a living and raising a family just like all our friends. George didn't talk about his past much, just little one-liners such as, "You don't know what it's like to be hungry. I was so hungry, I ate wood," or "I stood in the snow for hours with big holes in my shoes and no socks, no coat."

He was thrilled with our first apartment which consisted of two rooms in a basement with steam pipes running across the ceiling. To him, it was great. He had a place to hang his toothbrush and it would always be there, right in its place, right where he put it, waiting for him. He marveled for months that he could go to the refrigerator and take anything he wanted at any time. It all belonged to him. His goal was to have his own family and home, and this we accomplished.

George made -- and makes -- friends easily and has always been the proverbial optimist. He considered everyone a friend unless proven otherwise. On one of our first dates while walking through downtown Winona, he stopped and had a twenty minute conversation with a falling down drunk musician who was draped over a parking meter. I was totally embarrassed but that showed me what the future would be. He can just as easily talk to a dog or a child or a teenager, a president or a stranger, and truly enjoy and trust them all.

As our children grew, I wanted him to teach them German and he said no. As he told me bits about his past, I wanted him to tell the kids but he again said no, they were too young. They remained "too young" even as they left home for college and didn't know much about him or his family or his past.

The kids begged him to write things down so they would know their heritage. Finally, in the early 1990's, since he is a talker and not a writer, he agreed to tape his memories. I drew up a loose outline of his life and we began. All the tapes were made at our cabin in the north woods. Every evening, I would put dinner in the oven, get our drinks ready, George would light up a cigar, and we'd begin. I'd ask one question such as, "What do you remember about Ursula being born?" and he would start talking. His thoughts naturally were somewhat disorganized, one line of thought flowing into another. Sometimes he had good thoughts, but more often not. Sometimes it was so terrible, he had to stop.

At the end of that summer, my friend Wendy transcribed the tapes and there they sat in a drawer until we returned from the most significant event, the 50th Anniversary trip to Trobitz, commemorating the anniversary of the Lost Transport for survivors of that train ride and their families. You will read all about it. He returned from that trip a new man – a free man, reborn, uplifted, freed from the burden of fear, shame, and guilt.

One of the results of that is George's willingness now to tell his story.

Part One -- Lippstadt, Germany:
The Casting Out

Lord, who shall dwell in thy tabernacle or who shall rest upon thy holy hill?

He that hath used no deceit in his tongue, nor done evil to his neighbour.

(Prayer Book, 15: 1)

Lippstadt, Germany 1939

The last time I saw my mother was a cold, gray February morning in 1939, at a German railway station, I'm not even sure which one, possibly Lippstadt, my home town, or possibly Bielefeld, a neighboring town. My mother had helped my three year old sister, Ursula, and me pack a bag that morning as though we were going off on a little vacation to visit relatives in Holland.

Many children waited for the train accompanied mostly by their mothers. The scene was somber, but not hysterical by any means. All these Jewish mothers were there to put their children on what came to be known as the Kindertransport which would take a train load of children west to Rotterdam. The plan, of course, for us and I'm sure for all the kids, called for us to meet up with our mothers whenever they could take care of last minute business and make their way to Holland.

At the age of eight, however, I had seen some things already. I had seen our family home and business taken away. And I had seen my father and Uncle Ludwig die after being detained for several weeks by SS soldiers. So, although I believed my mother when she said she would see us soon, I was also worried. And I had my little sister to be responsible for. I remember crying. Getting out of Germany was by now difficult and my mother was able to get us on

1

this train through the intervention of a friend of hers with political influence. My mother, I remember, was crying and said to us, "Don't worry. I'm coming soon. Take care of your little sister."

Ursula and I took our seat on the train, and I waved and watched my mother as the train pulled away and she grew smaller and smaller, finally disappearing altogether. I never saw her again. Now, more than sixty years later, not a day goes by that I don't think of this, one of the great sad days of my life.

Her name was Lucie Hope Levy.

Lucie Hope married Max Levy, and they had only the two children, Ursula and myself, George Levy. I was born September 3, 1930. Memories of my early childhood are characterized by their utter normalcy. My life consisted of family, friends, and life in this small town on the River Lippe, Lippstadt. We were pretty well off, I remember, and had, for instance, a live-in maid who did most of the cooking.

The house I grew up in was – and still is – an impressive Bavarian style building on the corner of Kappelstrasse and Rathausstrasse. It was a big four story house with gables and bay windows and the clothing and dry goods store on the first floor with the living quarters above. Our family lived upstairs, and I remember my Grandfather Levy living with us on the floor above that.

One picture postcard taken probably around 1910 actually shows my Uncle Ludwig standing on the edge of the curb in front of the store, the sign above him indicating my grandfather's name, L.Levy. Ludwig stands at attention almost, arms locked behind his back, straw hat precisely balanced on his head, facing the camera. The narrow cobblestone street at his feet has only bicycle traffic to contend with and the buildings across the street are smaller clapboard and red tiled roofed homes and businesses.

The scene is very much one of a solid German Jewish merchant proudly situating himself before the family business. My family were German patriots and my father served in the German Army during World War I and earned the Iron Cross. His brother George died in action in WWI in France, and I was named after him. My mother's father and brothers were also in the German service. My family had an established place in the society and life of Lippstadt. And this solid sense of place, of belonging, was simply part of who I was the first few years. Children don't think about this – they just incorporate it naturally, like the air they breathe. The best I can tell you is the neighborhood was as normal and safe as the one I live in now in Glen Ellyn, Illinois. Just like we have neighbors and friends we are friendly with now, we had then.

One occasion that I always looked forward to with mixed emotions was when Uncle Joseph Mueller came to town. Uncle Joseph, a distinguished man with a lively eye, was my non-Jewish uncle by marriage and I loved being around him. Medical specialists were rare in those days, but he was a doctor specializing in obstetrics and gynecology. He married my mother's sister, Tante Irmgard. These sisters, though, were nothing alike. Tante Irmgard had a stern, strict attitude toward children and thought nothing of making us sit at the table for hours until we finished our meal. I'm sure she had a good heart as later on she, along with my uncle, provided us a home.

Cars were rare for people to own back then and my family, whose home and work were all in the same building, didn't need one. But Uncle Joseph came to town in his car and, boy, I was fascinated by this. We jokingly called his car a Deutsche Kinder Wagon – a German Kiddie Wagon – but it was a DKW. I think Audi evolved from that because they had those four rings in the grill.

I loved playing in the car while the adults were in the house visiting. I would start it up, lurch it into gear, then stop it abruptly, and repeat the process over and over, probably not doing the transmission a lot of good. Uncle Joseph never cared, never got mad at me for doing that. I loved riding in it so much that when they'd leave, I'd ride with them to the edge of town, then say goodbye and walk back home. Uncle Joseph and Tante Irmgard would drive home to Osnabruk which seemed far at the time, but was probably like Chicago to Milwaukee.

My mother went to Osnabruk so Uncle Joseph could deliver my sister, born May 11, 1935. He drove her along with the rest of us back to Lippstadt from Osnabruk and she cried all the way. Now my father, mother, sister, grandfather, and I lived in the big house over the store plus one more person – Uncle Ludwig, my father's brother. Uncle Ludwig was slow, probably somewhat retarded, so he lived with us and worked with my father helping out in the store. I was five when my sister was born and seven when my grandfather died passing the house and business along to my father. Grandfather's funeral and burial were traditionally Jewish. We honored these Jewish traditions, keeping mostly kosher (but not using all the separate dishes required) and attending temple on high holy days. But I would not describe us as having a highly religious orientation in our family.

One of my favorite family stories details how my Uncle Paul, my mother's brother, showed up at the house for the funeral of Grandfather Levy, accompanied by Aunt Irmgard, his and my mother's sister. Uncle Paul had driven his motorcycle and Tante Irmgard had ridden on the back. They arrived all very dusty. My mother opened the door and here was Uncle Paul in a rented tuxedo and a high hat. This vision struck my mother as hopelessly funny, and she had the worst kind of laughing attack imaginable, completely uncontrollable. As the laughing attack continued, people began to get mad at her. She tried to hide her laughing from my father who, naturally, was sad at his own father's funeral. All through the funeral, my mother was just shaking with laughter, but she tried to pass it off as crying. Grandfather Levy's funeral procession went from the synagogue to the cemetery, and the family business passed to the next generation.

The store itself held a conglomeration of smells and textures with its array of materials with which to make suits

4

and dresses. The well turned out Lippstadt family could get its materials, shirts, linens, gloves, and ties, among other necessities, from L. Levy's. He extended credit to local farmers, everyone who needed it, not just Jews. This was rare to give credit like my father did back then, and he was well liked and respected.

My father had this social life that included going to the local tavern. It's still there. My childhood friend, Hans Boenicke, told me he can remember the noise of the bowling alley every night and the sound of the beer glasses. My father loved to go there each night and drink beer, smoke, and bowl with his friends. These were other businessmen and friends from the community – not only Jews. German bowling is done with a smaller ball than American bowling. You can hold the ball in your hand. It's hard, like an American bowling ball, and moves swiftly down the raised track when the hard surface hits the wood. Hard balls moving down wooden tracks, beer steins plunking down on tables, men's voices raised in conversation in a smoke filled tavern – these were the pleasant sounds and smells of friends unwinding in the evenings. Whenever my father couldn't make it, he'd send me with a stein to bring back beer for him. He liked his beer.

My life was as normal as could be. My two best friends were Friedel Meyer whose parents owned a bakery down the street and Hans Boenicke whose parents owned a cutlery store – all three of us the sons of town merchants. Friedel owns his father's bakery today and Hans took over his father's store, then retired, and his son now runs it. Our store was taken, as I mentioned earlier, eventually through forced sale.

My father, the veteran, my mother, the popular, fun person, and our merchant family, had roots in this community for at least a century. This security defined my early life. Then I started noticing changes here and there. All of a sudden, people in our neighborhood wouldn't talk to my mother anymore. I remember one time I brought up the fact that a woman in the neighborhood who used to be friendly wasn't talking to my mother anymore. I was out on the street. My mother happened to be looking out of the second story window. She gave me the sternest look imaginable, her square jaw set, a wide eyed glare clearly warning me – I can still see that look she gave me. The message was clear: she absolutely did not want me to talk about this. I believe it was out of fear for our safety by that time.

I started noticing signs all over on billboards about Jewish people having big noses, and I remember they were pictured as having glasses on and their noses were like big hooks and snot would be coming out of their noses. I used to ask my mother what that was all about – is that what we look like? – and she always passed it off. I was in the second grade, around seven.

Just like we have the Cub Scouts, they had a thing over there called the Jung Volk which would be like the Cub Scouts, and the Hitler Youth which would be like the Boy Scouts. My best friends, Friedel and Hans, joined the Jung Volk along with other kids we played with. So I did, too.

During the short time I was part of the Jung Volk, I remember, they made us run and do calisthenics and made us jump off what seemed like a mountain into the unknown. We didn't know what was on the other side, and I was scared. They were trying to train us to be tough and follow orders. They'd make us run up the hill and jump over something, and we couldn't tell how far down we were jumping. It was probably nothing but it was frightening. And I remember I did it.

Then, the troop leader would come and talk to us. He'd say the Jews – they're no good. They're animals. Everyone would be looking at me, and I couldn't understand it. The next day, when I showed up, I was told I couldn't be a member. I was only a member for a couple days. I didn't know the political implications. I was just a little kid who was going to join the Cub Scouts. My parents said don't worry about it. That's what they said when other women wouldn't speak to my mother. And when my father could no longer go to the tavern. Don't worry about it.

I noticed a few other changes, like in school. I was in the Catholic school. My parents chose it because it was the best school around. During religion class, they made me go outside and wait on the playground. When I got back in class, they told me I killed Christ. I said, "I did?" Well, you didn't, I was told, but your people did.

Someone wearing a uniform would come in and give lectures. This uniform was the uniform of the SA who were the original "brown shirts" before the SS. The lectures were always against the Jews – it's all they ever talked about.

Naturally, I started feeling bad. I wasn't welcome anywhere, and I felt really strange as a little kid. I now wonder how people could make little kids feel that way.

Our family at that time had no real sense of ultimate danger and urgency. However, my Uncle Joseph did. He attended a medical meeting in Osnabruk and witnessed another doctor leap onto a table, draw a sword, and declare, "Das Judische blut muss fliessen" – "Jewish blood must flow." Uncle Joseph, extremely shaken by this display, left the meeting and drove directly to Lippstadt. He talked to my parents and told them, "You must get out." But my father could not believe that all our lives were in danger. After all, he was a German war veteran and his family were German merchants who were respected and part of town life for generations. They were, or felt they were, German to the core.

Uncle Joseph, however, fled Germany for the first time with his wife, Tante Irmgard. They were able to leave legally at that time and went to Brazil. Tante Irmgard, however, was unable to adjust to life there and insisted that they come home. So, back to Osnabruk they came, and by the time they fled again, they had to cross borders illegally.

One day, our family had to sell our house. They didn't literally take it away, but city authorities just came and told my father that he had to sell it and get out, and he actually sold it for pennies on the dollar, really giving it away. Let's just say the people who acquired it got a "good deal." They had a big sale and everything was gone in two or three days. People came in and bought all the clothes and fabrics. My Uncle Ludwig was there and they were all really busy. People were saying how sad it was that this was happening to Max Levy who was such a good guy. He was the only one that gave people credit. They could come into his store and buy a suit of clothing and fabric and wouldn't have to pay right then. Now they were basically taking it all away from him. No matter how sad people seemed, they still got their goods at a bargain price. And, of course, at this point all debts to my father's business were cancelled. The family home, assets, and income were gone. And we all went to the Lichtenfels who had a house designated by the Nazis for Jews to live in.

You know, the concentration camps were horrifying, as the world acknowledges now, and my experiences later in the camps were almost unimaginable. But not enough is said about how awful, how traumatic, being thrown out of your home and having everything taken away was. Imagine someone coming to your house and ordering you to leave and simply taking your bank accounts and valuables. In many ways, I think this was the worst, the very worst of the Holocaust experience, because it is so shocking, so unfathomable to disrupt totally the security of home.

Things pretty much went down hill from there.

After we lost the house and business, we simply had no where to go. We were literally homeless. So, our little family – Mother, Father, Uncle Ludwig, Ursula, and I – went to live with a Jewish family in town named Lichtenfels. My father ended up purchasing this house, and the Lichtenfels were then able to escape to the United States. Judging by their lifestyle, the Lichtenfels must have been well to do. For instance, they had two cars, a chauffeur, and a garage while our family, reasonably well off, had no car. They took us in, I would guess, as my memory is not precise here, in the fall of 1938. I can't even remember if I continued to attend school during this time. But one day, my mother told me that the Nazis had taken my father and Uncle Ludwig away. This coincided with Kristallnacht, the first official, mass government pogram. Kristallnacht, the "night of broken glass," took place on November 9 - 10, 1938. Many German businesses, homes, and synagogues were destroyed and burned. Thousands of Jews were beaten, arrested, harassed, and detained all over Germany.

The Nazis took my father and uncle to a concentration camp near Oranienburg called Sachsenhausen near Berlin. We have now come into possession of a copy of the Nazi records showing when my father and Uncle Ludwig were processed in and out of Sachsenhausen. This treatment was part of organized harassment that preceded actual policies of extermination. A few weeks later, my father and uncle were sent home. The Nazi documentation shows the date of release from the camp of my father and Uncle Ludwig as December 22, 1938. But my father came back on a stretcher. The prisoners themselves carried him home, and my Uncle Ludwig walked from the train station. Three days later, Uncle Ludwig died at the Lichtenfels house where he and my father both returned. My father was also in bad shape. I went to see him, and he was sitting on a dresser crying. He said he couldn't use his legs. They had been frozen while at the camp when he was forced to stand for long periods of time in snow, which led to gangrene and septic, oozing sores. He had big sores all over his body and he kind of talked to me, as I recall. He put his hand on me and even then tried to reassure me that things were going to be all right. Shortly, he was taken away to the Catholic hospital in Lippstadt and we went to visit him – my mother, my sister, and myself – but he had his back turned to us and was unable to say much. The next day in the Lichtenfels' living room, my mother told me he was dead. He died January 12, 1939. She asked me if I wanted to see him, but I said no. I did not want to see my father dead. He was buried in the Jewish cemetery in a regular, Jewish service, in the same cemetery as Uncle Ludwig.

I was about eight and a half years old at this time.

Not long after these deaths, my mother received a letter from her half brother, Uncle Rudolph. Uncle Rudolph had managed to flee to Argentina earlier. His letter said that she should leave Germany, that it was important for her to get out. Mother respected Uncle Rudolph greatly and decided to take his advice, but couldn't make the arrangements to leave just yet. So, this is when she made arrangements for Ursula and me to leave for the Netherlands. A friend of hers helped my mother with her affairs after my father died. Rumor had it that he admired her. Most importantly, he had some kind of political influence, so he made the arrangements for Ursula and me to go to Holland. Perhaps now, seeking safety in Holland seems ironic considering that we know now that Holland's Jewish population was one of the most devastated of the war, but back then it seemed to offer an alternative to what was happening in Germany.

So it happened when the Kindertransport pulled out of the station, Ursula and I were on it heading into Holland.

Lippstadt, Germany 2000

Our white rented minivan crossed the River Lippe, and we caught sight of the narrow, green river, overhanging branches touching the water from the wooded shore. The Lippe is a river too small for sport boating and much too small for commercial navigation, but plenty big enough to draw young boys to its banks for fishing, perhaps, or whatever games are on the young-boy agenda that day. No evidence of a swift current or anything dangerous lurks there. The river, important enough to give the town its name many generations ago, does not dominate the down town, but rather meanders its way through back yards away from the small town's busy center. On the map, Lippstadt isn't far from Celle and Celle is located very near the little towns of Bergen and Belsen, a fact not incidental to this story.

The doors flew open as the mini-van dislodged its six American passengers more interested for the moment in stretching legs and locating rooms and restrooms at the Drei Kronen, the old inn holding our reservations. We had driven from Amsterdam this afternoon and at least the women were willing to admit to still reeling from the non-stop entertainment of the autobahn. For the fortunately uninitiated, the term "autobahn" is simply the German term for their limited access highway system like U.S. freeways. But the autobahn is unencumbered by speed limits. If you can picture German engineered sedans, Mercedes Benzes, Audis, and Passats tailgating one another, slip streaming really, at a good 100 mph and up, you've captured an image of the autobahn. The occasionally glimpsed piece of bumper or side view mirror or unidentifiable car part appeared and disappeared near the center divide in a flash of sunlight off disembodied chrome. After this bit of stressful travel, we were anxious to find our rooms.

The woman who welcomed us at the Drei Kronen spoke to us in English. All others who worked here spoke only German. The check-in procedure was a remarkably casual affair. She passed out keys and told us we could figure out the bills later. My roommate Sue and I were directed to a third floor room and accordingly schlepped our backpacks up the old stairs. We were simultaneously delighted and dismayed by what we found – delighted at the space available to us in the form of two bedrooms, a hallway, and a bathroom, and dismayed at the fact the rooms hadn't been cleaned since the last patrons. Sue's window overlooked a scenic town square made of bricks and situated in front of an old city hall. I opened a desk drawer and found an empty whiskey pint staring back at me. I closed the drawer leaving it undisturbed. The pint bottle well could have been there for years. This disconcerting blend of past and present would characterize our stay in Lippstadt.

The six of us met downstairs a few minutes later. We had all come to Lippstadt to see the town where George spent the first eight years of his life. We had come to

Germany to see if being on site could help us breathe in George's Holocaust experience, make us understand it more. Could we conjure up the hellish spirits that lived side by side with good memories? And where, individually, would each of us sense that spirit? Our party consisted of 69 year old George Levy Mueller, his wife of more than forty years, Katie, their daughter Amy and her husband, Dan, another daughter Sue, and me, friend of Sue, along primarily to observe and record. Our plan was to walk around Lippstadt while George showed us old haunts, find a place for dinner, get a good night's rest, and then meet his childhood chum, Hans Boenicke, for breakfast the next morning. George's triple threat command of English, German, and Dutch kept his five language impaired companions functional.

We met on the sidewalk out front and didn't have to even move from the spot to take in the first image of George's memory. "That square there," he said pointing across the street to the town square visible from Sue's room, "that's where I saw a Nazi rally. It must have been around 1935. It didn't mean much to me then. I was just a little kid. But there was music – which I loved – and it was something to do. Everyone, it seemed, gathered in the square."

We thought about the Nazis being, somehow, just another political party, like a Republican or Democratic rally in the United States. Was this what political rallies were like to the people of Lippstadt back then? George is only sure of the circus of it – an event, some music. I took pictures of George and his family in the square. One finds the small victories among the devastation when re-visiting the Holocaust and the fact that Hitler was long dead but that George and his children who all had children of their own were alive and standing in this square was one of those victories worth recording.

George Levy Mueller looks younger than his 69 years. At 5'6", he carries around 150 pounds and is always looking for a way to trim what he considers that extra five pounds. George is aware of fashion and always looks dapper. He sports a good looking leather aviator's jacket which is more than a fashion statement. It's an identity as well. George is a pilot who loves to fly small aircraft when he has the chance. He owns a sporty cap which he wears with panache. He has just enough of a streak of male vanity to make him interesting but not enough to make him obnoxious, and he enjoys cigars and a drink although nothing to excess. As a still-working pharmacist, he's also health conscious and routinely runs several miles a day. His indulgences are moderate and occasional and, therefore, enjoyed all the more.

George enjoys nothing so much as a good laugh, and he doesn't discriminate on the source. His sense of humor runs from low to high, and he is as quick with an easy scatological joke as with a witty bit of word play. He remarks often on the necessity of seeing the jokes around us, acknowledging the humor of life. He's a firm believer in a positive outlook as a survival mechanism.

All of these things make him an easy traveling companion. But, still and all, the purpose of this trip isn't tourism although we manage some sight seeing. Rather, we've come to retrace and establish a sense of place to George's family history and their Holocaust experiences. Lippstadt is the starting point of establishing this sense of place and of George who was born here. George's good humor gives way to a darker mood almost as soon as we drive into Germany from Holland. Lippstadt is not his favorite place to be, he's made clear to us. Although visiting Lippstadt is a new experience for Amy, Sue, Dan, and me, George has been here since the war. Most notably, he and Katie, their daughters Lucy and Jane, and son Joe and his wife Maureen, came in 1995 when the fiftieth anniversary of the end of the war was commemorated. This anniversary trip, as the children and Katie who participated in it will describe in the last chapter of this book, was significant in many ways including allowing George, for the first time, he said, to talk freely about his experiences during the Holocaust. Since then, he has agreed that these memories are worth recording

We all had the stories of George's upbringing and loss in mind as we wandered Lippstadt on a Saturday night. Shops were closed but bars and restaurants were still open. The six of us had spent the previous day and even this particular morning in Amsterdam being regular tourists before our drive to Lippstadt. We went to Anne Frank's house (in many ways anticipatory of George's story), the Reijks Museum, the Van Gogh Museum, took a canal boat ride, and ogled in amazement at the beautiful flowers of Keukenhof. We bought tulip bulbs and postcards and took a touristy peek at the brown bars and red light district. But we knew this was all a pleasant interlude to getting down to the real business of the trip.

Lippstadt is like many small German towns, well tended and clean. You won't see trash thrown along the sidewalks or yards. People keep gardens all over. All the words apply that tourists use to describe such towns – quaint, old-world (since it's in the "old world"), cute. The Dutch language that we were starting to get used to hearing in Holland had now given way to the more guttural, harsher sound of German.

A few short blocks down from the town square, we found ourselves at the corner of George's old family home. An insurance company now, apparently, occupied the first floor, and the building had obviously been divided into a few apartments judging by the several mailboxes hanging there. The innkeeper had informed George that this property was worth maybe two million dollars today. We couldn't tell who owned it.

George looked up toward the bay window. He was trying to remember how many floors the family really used as living space. He recalled that there was a big table the family used in the bay window room and that the Christmas before the end, his father had thrown a fur coat across the table, an extravagant gift to his wife who loved fashionable clothes. The prosperous merchant enjoyed such moments and could afford them.

All of us stood looking up at this building trying to imagine these days. We asked George if he wanted to ring any of the apartments, ask anyone to let him in to look around. Emphatically, he did not. Perhaps he did not need to be inside to recreate his childhood memories; perhaps he did not want to be a guest in his own home. His comment about standing in front of his family home: "One part of me wants to ring the bell and tell everyone to get the hell out. The other part of me just wants to say let's get the hell out of here."

We stood on the street talking quietly about the past. The bon vivant George of Amsterdam was now a quietly spoken George of Lippstadt. He practically lowered his voice to a whisper and when the word "Jew" was used, he was quieter still. I couldn't help but be aware of the mild, almost subtle scent of sewage hinting at the infrastructure of this pretty little town. Dan asked George if the town had sustained bombing damage during the war. George wasn't sure of the extent of any damage from this but his sentiments were clear: "They should have bombed this place off the face of the earth."

George could, and did, have very logical and rational thoughts about the notions of national character versus historical circumstance, individual characteristics versus the collective. He could, and did, discuss individual Germans he loved and respected: his Uncle Joseph being a prime one; his friend Hans Boenicke another. At the same time, he commented repeatedly: "Give the Germans a chance and they'll try it again – to take over the world. Just give them a chance." Yet, back in the United States, George was often heard to distinguish between the average German citizen and the Nazis. But standing on the corner looking at his old home, one could understand the thoughts he expressed. These thoughts colored every exchange we had with the Germans during our brief stay. It was just the nature of the trip, and all the rest of us were surprised how it influenced our own personal impressions.

15

We found a good restaurant along the main street for dinner that night not more than two blocks from the old Levy home. (Our trip standard for good restaurants was based mostly on glancing through windows to see if there were table cloths.) George had the considerable task of translating an extensive menu to the other five of us. Of course, once wasn't enough. We all had him repeat numerous items as we would forget what we were comparing with what as we went along. Not surprisingly, George got a bit bored with this at some point and small whines of "George" or "Dad, read number 32 again," wafted across the table. But we all had beer and it was good. George would talk to the proprietor in German and, like most people we encountered, he quickly figured out George was a native. But George was not forthcoming with the locals regarding his connection to the town.

We had decided during dinner to look for the old bowling alley bar that Max Levy frequented almost every night. By process of elimination, George figured out which building had to be the one. Now it was a nice restaurant. We took a look inside and George talked to the likely owner. He asked about the presence of a bowling alley here and the reaction was one of irritation and immediate denial on the part of the proprietor. He swished us away with his hands, shaking his head. No bowling alley here. George's memory must not be clear on this point.

Wakeful and curious later that night, however, Amy and Dan returned to the spot. Their persistence paid off. Not only was this the right location, there was still a bowling alley in the back room, no doubt where Max Levy and his friends bowled each night. Speaking only English might have been an advantage for Amy and Dan because at some point, the proprietor, apparently tired of them, waved them to the back. A private party was in progress. They were invited to sit down with the group and have a drink. They were even allowed to snap some pictures. The earlier discomfort of the owner remains a curiosity.

We were all looking forward to the next morning. Hans Boenicke and his wife Laurie were going to meet us for breakfast at the Drei Kronen. Hans, the childhood friend of George's, was taking time out to talk to us knowing our purpose. He's two years older than George and has lived in this town all his life taking over the family store and then passing it along to his son. This is the legacy and the stability of the merchant class in Lippstadt.

Sue and I arrived for breakfast to find Amy and Dan already seated with a German couple – obviously Hans and Laurie – and everyone was smiling politely but no one was talking. The Boenicke's clearly spoke no English and . . . well, as to us, George wasn't there yet. I came equipped with the usual tape recorder, camera, and notebook. A waitress poured coffee and indicated a buffet table to us.

Soon, in came George and Katie. Hans and George literally glowed in each other's presence. Like two old friends anywhere who hadn't seen each other for some time, they clearly were comparing signs of aging. Even in German, we could see that Hans obviously told George he looked young and in response, George patted the back of his head and turned, indicating some thinning hair. They looked each other up and down, a happy reunion. Hans is a big man with white hair and a ruddy complexion. His clear, shimmering blue eyes add intensity to the conversation, and he talks with such expression and gestures that he seems to will the meaning of his words across the table, often with success. His wife, wearing a neat skirt and blouse, is a quiet, petite, and attractive woman with gray hair. She's clearly less comfortable with all of this but game nonetheless. She's glad to see Katie, another petite, neatly dressed woman closer to her age. George introduced everyone. Hans brought George a gift of several books, one being a history of the Jews of Lippstadt.

Hans, it turns out, has had an interest for the last several years in story telling in the oral tradition as a way of both keeping history alive and making it entertaining so that people will want to learn. This is a lucky break for us because Hans is articulate and generous with his memories. For the next two hours, Hans fills in George's Lippstadt story as well as telling some of his own.

On some issues where George's memory is fuzzy, Hans' memory is clear. Hans attended the Lutheran school in town while George attended St. Nicolai, the Catholic school. Hans recollects with assurance that George, upon release from school each day, headed over to the Hebrew school at the synagogue, a memory that isn't clear to George.

When the political climate changed in town, everyone was affected. Hans was expected to be part of the Hitler youth organization, the Jung Volks, from which George had been summarily disinvited. Early in their childhood, the differences in their religion, in the matter of being Jewish or non-Jewish, were incidental, not worth much consideration. Hans, Friedel, and George were all three the best of friends, as young boys are.

The parents were close as well. The two families joined each other for picnics and the parents played games together and visited after the children were in bed. When the climate changed, everyone in town became fearful. At some point, the parents decided it was dangerous for the children to play together, and Hans and Friedel were forbidden to play with George. Both George and Hans recalled that they found opportunities anyway because they were just kids with no understanding of the larger situation.

Hans recollects Kristallnacht in Lippstadt: The Nazis came and burned down the synagogue. The local firemen assembled to put out the fire but were barred by the Nazis and so everyone stood watching the synagogue burn to the ground. Today there is a house on the site of the synagogue and the only reminder is a plaque with the Star of David on it explaining that the Lippstadt synagogue used to be here but was burned during Kristallnacht. After the war, there simply were never enough Jews living in Lippstadt again to rebuild. Even now, Hans estimates only a very small number of Jewish families live in Lippstadt.

18

While this time period was devastating to the Levy family – having lost their home and then Max and Ludwig being killed – non-Jewish citizens of Lippstadt like the Boenicke's were having some difficulties as well. Hans' father was overheard telling a political joke about Hitler. That afternoon, a policeman came to the Boenicke house and arrested him. Hans was playing at the local sports field when his two maiden aunts showed up to tell him what happened. He knew it was something bad to bring them out to the field. Luckily, Herr Boenicke was friends with the town mayor who authorized his release.

Lucie Levy, then living with a cousin in Olde fifty miles from Lippstadt, came back to town to visit her friend, Frau Boenicke, when George and Ursula were in Holland. A beautiful, fashionably dressed Lucie arrived at the Boenicke home wearing a large hat to hide her face and identity. The disguise was not good enough, however, and her presence in the home was reported. Hans is sure the neighborhood snitches were a family of poor people who lived right across from the Levy's. The Levy's used to give them food and clothes, but they were noted for snooping on their wealthier neighbors with a spy glass. At any rate, the town newspaper published the report of Lucie's visit with headlines the next day: "Frau Boenicke Entertains the Jewess Levy." Hans was taunted on his way to school by talk of his mother appearing in the paper.

He hurried to his Wednesday Hitler Youth meeting early that afternoon because he knew the paper would be posted. Grabbing a chair, he sat with his back to the wall hiding the headlines of his mother and Lucie's visit. An SS friend of Frau Boenicke's later reported to her that there was talk of tearing her out of her home and parading her in the street for being a Jew lover. Hans' mother, who never normally bought the paper, bought this one and saved it until just before the Americans liberated Lippstadt. She burned it then out of fear. After the newspaper incident, Lucie could no longer visit the Boenicke home. To this day, this fact more than anything else that happened to the Levy family brings tears to Hans' eyes.

Hans, himself, was drafted into Hitler's army at the age of sixteen. All of us talked about kids we knew who were sixteen, considering how young this really is. He was sent to the Western front. By the age of seventeen, he surrendered and was an American held prisoner of war. His confusion at being in the army was intense: "On the one hand, I was German and wanted to help Germany. On the other hand, I knew some things that were happening weren't right." He assumed that once you surrendered, you were no longer enemies but was to discover this was not necessarily so. Upset that some of his possessions were stolen, he complained and an American officer ordered that they be returned. He has no complaints about his treatment as a prisoner of war. At age eighteen, the war was over, and he was back in Lippstadt rebuilding the family business with his father. We all thought about the different paths that befell the Levy's and the Boenicke's.

At the end of breakfast, the old friends posed for pictures and gave each other an affectionate good-bye. Hans is not yet on e-mail, the modern way for George to keep in touch with all his friends and acquaintances in Europe. Oddly, we all felt somewhat sad and disconnected to hear that Hans has no e-mail address.

As I gathered my possessions together to check out of the Drie Kronen, I thought about George's son, Joe, who had visited Lippstadt five years earlier. Joe swiped a bottle opener from the hotel in Lippstadt as a symbol of taking something back from the town that seemed to have stolen so much. I understood the gesture and wondered if we might not be staying in the same room as there was no bottle opener here. There was nothing else we were willing to grab. I glanced once more at the empty whiskey pint and closed the door behind me.

We piled into the van, beginning now to have a system of packing and seating that seemed to suit everyone. We had one more task in Lippstadt – to locate Max Levy's

20

grave. George on previous trips had visited the cemetery but had been unable to find it. After some false starts and stops around town, we came to the municipal cemetery. (Imagine how things change in fact and in imagination if you hadn't lived in a town since you were nine years old. Earlier when George asked directions as we headed to Lippstadt, his question came out some amalgam of German and English. His frustration was evident: "Damn! I can't talk any more!" Frequent use of three languages in two days can do that.)

We parked and headed off to locate the Jewish section of the cemetery. Katie suggested asking someone, but George said, "Don't ask." After a short time, we came to the section marked by Stars of David and began wandering up and down the rows. Clearly, this section of the cemetery wasn't so big that we couldn't look at each and every grave if we needed to.

The German graves were very different from what we were used to in the United States. In keeping with the intensive gardening we had seen all over, each grave was a small garden with various flowers and plants growing over the entire grave apparently planted and tended by the individual surviving families. They are beautiful and eccentric, none like its neighbor. We took all this in as we finished our search for the Jewish sector.

The first marker with a familiar name on it was a World War I memorial to Jewish veterans from Lippstadt and George's uncle's name was there. Then down the row a way, we came across the grave of Ludwig Levy, Uncle Ludwig. The grave, with no more Levys in Lippstadt to attend to it, was overgrown and weedy, a relative eyesore compared to others . Before leaving, we did what we could pulling the weeds and overgrown grass away and at least giving the grave a neat appearance.

Dan hollered that he had found Max's grave and indeed he had. We all hurried over to see. The reason George had been unable to find the grave before was because a bush had literally overgrown and obliterated the site. But Dan, knowing about where it should be, persisted and located the grave. Someone produced a knife and trimmed away at the bush clearing the grave in much the same way Uncle Ludwig's had been cleared.

George and his family had their pictures taken at what appeared to be their father and grandfather's grave. It was a somber moment and we were all glad that George had at least this satisfaction. George translated the marker that his sister Ursula had ordered many years ago:

> To Our Dear Parents –
> Max Levy, died January 12, 1939.
> Lucie Levy, died 1944 in the concentration camp at Stuthoff.
> Ludwig Levy, died December 25, 1938.

Of these three names, only Max's remains had been buried in this spot. Only a memorial remained for Lucie, and the name of the concentration camp gave a clue to her fate that George had not had the heart to investigate more fully until now. He had thought Lucie died at Riga but now wasn't sure. He would find more answers about Lucie when he returned home. Ludwig's grave was a couple rows over. George and Katie said they would have to try to take care of this from home.

The marker also said, "Rest in Peace." We placed stones on the grave and left Lippstadt behind.

Part Two -- Eersel, Holland: Temporary Refuge

Nowhere to go but out,

Nowhere to come but back.

(Benjamin Franklin King. Jr.
"The Pessimist")

Things went downhill from there.

(George Levy Mueller)

Holland 1939

Now that I reflect on it, I realize that my years in Holland were all spent essentially hiding out, you might say, even though most of this time it was in plain sight. But my desire and attitude during these war years caused me to see my life as somewhat stable and as re-established in terms of nationality from German to Dutch. During my Holland years, 1939 – 1947, I came to speak Dutch with no trace of an accent and to this day, I consider myself Dutch, not German. Once the Kindertransport pulled into the station in Holland, the government, as yet a true, unoccupied Dutch government, took over our lives and attempted to provide for us as well as possible. In the end, of course, we were given up to the Nazis, but in the meantime, I began the process of finding some semblance of a predictable, normal life.

One might guess that my mother never came to Holland as planned. This is true and my knowledge of her fate eventually came to rely on rumors until after the war. But I did hear from her a few times via mail. She sent me postcards assuring me things would be all right and urging me to be good and to be nice to Ursula.

23

The Dutch government took in all these Jewish and half Jewish children and sent us to a place near Rotterdam called Hyplaat where a big displaced persons camp of Jewish people had been established. Those who were there with their whole family were often sent to Westerbork, another camp, instead. Because people were, in fact, concentrated there, Hyplaat was sort of like a concentration camp. But it was not an enemy concentration camp, and the Dutch took care of us the best they could. We had plenty to eat and they treated us well, but it was still a big camp, and we lived in a barracks and ate in a mess hall.

The Jewish people of the camp established a routine for the children that included regular schooling plus Hebrew school. I did learn some Hebrew while I was there, but I've since forgotten it. Adults living in the camp taught school.

I have more what you might call snapshot memories from my time at Hyplaat, rather than detailed, day to day memories. For instance, Hyplaat was located on the Rhine River, and I well remember the excitement of submarines coming through the camp. As a young boy, I was quite interested in this, and really everyone found it fascinating.

We had a recreation area that included a ping pong table and that's where I learned to play ping pong – in Hyplaat. We also had team sports, and I played soccer.

But I was a child who had been accustomed to a lot of family while growing up – my parents, uncles, aunts – and I was certainly homesick for my mother. One day, my Tante Sophie somehow sent for Ursula and me, and we spent a day with her and her husband, Uncle Albert. Tante Sophie was the sister of Uncle Rudolph who was by this time in Argentina. Tante Sophie and Uncle Rudolph were half siblings to my mother. Tante Sophie and Uncle Albert fled their home in Dusseldorf to live in Amsterdam as so many people had done.

So, my sister and I got to leave Hyplaat for a whole day to visit Tante Sophie and Uncle Albert. They gave us bread, butter, and strawberry jam for breakfast. And Tante Sophie gave me a bath. The plan may have originally been for Ursula and me to live with Tante Sophie and Uncle Albert but really the Dutch government had made provisions for all these children.

Living with my aunt and uncle in Amsterdam were more distant relatives that I called Uncle Julius and Tante Lise. Tante Lise and Uncle Julius actually had a car of their own, and I still have a picture of Tante Lise in their car, quite an unusual thing at the time.

They had a dog, a dachshund named Waldman ("woodsman"). Uncle Julius had him trained. He could put a piece of meat on the dog's nose, and he would say, "This is from Hitler." Waldman would leave this meat untouched on his nose. Then, Uncle Julius would say, "This is from Koenigin Wilhemena (Queen Wilhemena) from Holland," and then the dog would eat it.

These four people – Tante Sophie, Uncle Albert, Tante Lisa, and Uncle Julius – disappeared in the concentration camps. Sometimes I think, imagine these people just disappearing like that. And so much depends on decisions we have no control over. If we had gone to live with them, we no doubt would have disappeared too.

Exactly how long Ursula and I were in Hyplaat isn't clear to me now. Long enough for me to learn ping pong and Hebrew and to get into a routine of sorts. Then, all of a sudden – or so it seemed to me – Ursula and I were put on a train and sent to S'Hertogenbos which was commonly called Den Bos and is the capital of the Dutch state of Brabant. Now, this is where my Uncle Joseph's influence in my life becomes evident. Although he had tried without success to convince my father to flee Germany, he and Tante Irmgard got out and, most importantly, got far enough away, didn't stop in Holland. They had to go illegally the second time – after Tante Irmgard couldn't adjust to life in Brazil – and went by way of Holland, England, and eventually to the United States. By the time we were on the train to Den Bos, Uncle Joseph was in the United States.

For a while, Uncle Joseph had practiced medicine at a hospital in Den Bos and was held in great esteem. People

25

remembered him well at this hospital after he left, and I would come to learn this first hand later.

Apparently, my mother had relinquished her authority over us children in favor of Uncle Joseph who, in turn, directed a gentleman named Meneer v. Mackelenbergh to take care of us. Meneer v. Mackelenbergh took his charge seriously, fortunately for us, and began directing our future to the best of his ability.

Meneer v. Mackelenbergh was a distinguished and kindly man. He wore round glasses, had gentle eyes and a mustached upper lip. He was a thin man who stood erect.

Meneer v. Mackelenbergh met us in Den Bos and showed me around various places where my uncle and aunt had been, speaking highly of Uncle Joseph and Tante Irmgard. Meneer v. Mackelenbergh told me that he was in charge of Jewish children from Germany, and he was going to take care of us. He was acting as our guardian now. After spending one night in Den Bos, he sent us to a wonderful place, Eersel. Of course, at the time, I didn't see it as so wonderful. But it was a place I was to leave and come back to three times beyond my first arrival there over the course of the next several years. The name of this place was St. Jacobus and it was a koloniehuis – sort of a spa or camp for kids as well as a Catholic convent. The nuns ran the place. The purpose of St. Jacobus was to provide a place where deprived city kids from all over the Netherlands could get some good food and country life for six weeks at a time. There were maybe two hundred girls and two hundred boys living in separate quarters.

Around fifty of us were there in a protected capacity as refugees from the Nazis. Out of that fifty, most were half Jewish. Out of this population of half-Jews, all survived the war. Only three of us were all Jewish – Ursula, me, and Ilse Brul. Everyone else would come in, spend their six weeks enjoying country life, and leave. We'd get to be friends with someone and in six weeks they'd be out of there.

St. Jacobus was in all respects a remarkable place. Physically, St. Jacobus was an elaborate series of large, brick

26

buildings, two and three stories, with plenty of windows to allow for excellent light and ventilation. Girls' and boys' facilities were completely separate including playgrounds. The buildings were surrounded by beautiful grounds with large trees and hazelnut bushes. So, you can imagine, if you are facing St. Jacobus, on the right a two story, roomy house that served as the rectory for, during the time I was there, Father Leo Weyers. To the left of the rectory was a large, three story convent with a statue of St. Jacobus placed above the main entrance and set off with a gable in the middle of the roofline. The nuns, led by Mother Renildus, lived in the convent. Between the convent and the large facilities for the children was a two story staff house.

St. Jacobus was self-sufficient and state of the art regarding things like kitchen facilities. The St. Jacobus farm had cows and chickens and pigs, and fruit trees – apples, plums, cherries, pears, all this delicious fruit that I could help myself to. We grew our own strawberries. The convent baker, a man named Theis, turned home-made flour into wonderful baked goods. Then, in the kitchen, the dishes were actually washed by a huge, industrial sized dishwasher which seemed just as modern as one you'd find in a restaurant or hotel today. Clothes were dried in automatic dryers in the convent laundry. Racks pulled out from this dryer upon which clothes would be hung. Then, the racks would be inserted again inside the dryer and the clothes automatically dried. Everything was extremely modern. No expense seemed spared to create an excellent environment for the children of this koloniehuis.

The chapel on the grounds had a beautiful tower visible from anywhere at St. Jacobus. There was even an organist. Father Weyers served as chaplain. He was quite the athlete in his day, and I remember watching him skate, writing his name in the ice.

Father Weyers took a liking to my sister and me. We observed his lifestyle first hand because he invited us over. His apartment was large and well appointed, and one nun's full time job consisted of taking care of him. Ursula and I ate dinner with him once or twice a week. He was one of eight brothers who all became doctors, lawyers, professionals. When I visited there in 1954 while serving in the U.S. military, the nun who took care of Father Weyers cried and told me how much she missed him since he had passed away.

No matter how modern the surroundings or how favored we were in this setting, it was still an institutional life. Picture meals with two hundred boys lined up closely with one another at long tables with equally long benches to sit upon. The food was delicious, the room light and airy, but nonetheless, eating dinner with two hundred boys is not a homelike setting. Neither were the barracks-like sleeping arrangements.

But I settled into life at St. Jacobus and in the town of Eersel. Ursula and the other refugee girls were sent to the local girls' school in town, and I joined the boys in the local school where I was able to make friends with the Eersel boys who did not leave after six weeks. Sjef Blox, Ties Kwinten, Hans Raymakers, all the v.Dykes, including Mama v.Dyke who had one of the town bakeries, became my friends. We hung out at the v.Dyke's bakery and while I was with the town friends, life seemed normal, a world of families, businesses, and individuality impossible to find in even the best of institutions.

This part of Brabant was at that time very rural. My best friend, Sjef Blox, lived right across the street from St. Jacobus. My friends didn't enjoy all the modern conveniences of St. Jacobus. Sjef's family had a horse in the back yard going around in circles attached to a mill grinding grain. Sometimes we would ride the horse. When we walked into Sjef's house, we walked into the great room with exposed wooden beams dominated by a huge fireplace that I could easily stand in. The fire was the source of warmth and cooking. Rough bricks made up the floor. Plain wooden chairs, cane bottomed, ladder backed mostly, provided seating. Roofs on the local houses were commonly thatched looking the Dutch cottages they were. Farmers and their dogs were often seen shepherding flocks of sheep to pasture. The faces of the locals were prematurely weathered, deeply lined and tanned from hard work and exposure to the outdoors. They led hard working lives with few conveniences, but none of this mattered to me. I loved being at the Blox house. It was home where a family lived. It was normal. During the times I spent there, so was I.

At this time, toward the end of 1939, I began taking lessons at St. Jacobus in Catholicism, and I was baptized. Now the story goes that my mother wanted it this way. She had a propensity for the Catholic Church and used to sneak us to the Catholic church saying that, if my father ever died, she would convert to Catholicism. She, you might say, had a "thing" about the church. I think part of it had to do with saving herself, but some of it had to do with the mystery, the tradition, or maybe the music. I don't know. I don't know if she even knew that much about the Catholic church. But, anyway, we were baptized, and, then later at confirmation, I was given a middle name, Herman, after Uncle Herman, one of the chaplain's brothers. Uncle Herman and Tante Gonda lived in Tilburg. So, now I am Georg Herman Levy. And not only did I become a Catholic, but an altar boy like my best friend, Sjef. Nuns used the local boys as altar boys because of the quick turnover of the children normally staying at St. Jacobus.

Then, yet another significant shift took place which I was aware of but did not fully realize the implications of for my own safety. The Germans invaded Holland. The war for Holland lasted all of four days before the Germans won. Things started to change again. The first thing I noticed personally was that my bicycle -- I actually had a bicycle -- was taken by a German soldier. I continued my normal existence hanging out with Sjef, going to school, but now there were articles in the local newspaper about Jews, just like in Lippstadt earlier. The mayor of Eersel was replaced by another Dutchman, a member of the Dutch Nazi Party, the NSB, a guy I remember with a beard. But as a kid, I still wasn't that concerned because the war seemed to go on and on and that had become sort of normal, too.

However, the war got worse and worse. First English and later American airplanes would come over. In response, the Germans instituted blackouts, absolutely no light shining out of any window at night. They didn't want the town to be targets of Allied bombing raids. The nuns of St. Jacobus made cardboard window covers. At night, we would go over every window – and there were many – and place one of the cardboard covers over each window. If any light remained visible, the Germans came over and shot into the window. During this time, things got a little worse. More of the German/Jewish kids came and went, but we stayed.

Germans were goose stepping all over town in their hobnailed boots. These boots literally had nails out of the bottom of the soles, kind of like extreme spikes on golf shoes. Even one soldier could make a terrible racket walking, let alone marching, in those boots. Several soldiers sounded like a hundred. It was quite intimidating. The Dutch kept saying that the Allies were winning. I was a little bit concerned, but as a ten year old, I had no idea if this was going to have a big effect on me personally.

At this age, I would play everywhere I could manage. In the basement at St. Jacobus we had a boiler room, and one day I was exploring and opened the door to this room. There sat the first black man I had ever laid eyes on! I was startled. He scared the socks off me, and I ran straight upstairs and right smack into one of the nuns. She took me straight to Mother Renildus who asked me, "What did you see in the basement?" and I told her I had seen this black man. "No," she said, "You saw nothing." I told her again what I had seen but after the third time of her saying, "No, you saw nothing," I understood and never said anything to anyone. Mother Renildus, I came to know later, worked with the Dutch resistance. I guessed the man was a downed American flyer.

Mother Renildus was one of those people who was in the right place at the right time. Although the Church would have changed the head of St. Jacobus about every couple of years under normal conditions, everyone understood that Mother Renildus was the right person to keep on during the war. Although she wasn't as strict about religious details as some others, she had the political savvy to navigate through very tough times. Like Roosevelt or Churchill, she was the right person for that moment in history.

About this time, Meneer v. Mackelenbergh decided to send me to a school called The Ruwenberg. He pulled me out of the fourth or fifth grade that I was in and told me I was going to a better school. The Ruwenberg was an excellent boarding school run by the Catholic brothers of Tilburg, Holland.

They had three cours, or departments, at the school, Dutch, French, and English. Whichever department you were in as a student, you lived on that campus and spoke only that language, learning all your courses in that language. For instance, students in the French cour lived together, spoke only French, learned math, science, everything in French. In a couple years, students moved on to another cour. I was in the Dutch cour but didn't stay long enough to move to the French or English cour.

Like St. Jacobus, we showered in private stalls with our shorts on. These Catholic schools – St. Jacobus or The Ruwenberg – were very sexually repressive. For years, I assumed it was normal or at least expected to shower with shorts on.

During vacations, I returned to St. Jacobus where I saw my sister and my friends. A number of the German children had been dispersed from St. Jacobus but returned during vacations. So, for the first time since arriving, I went out from St. Jacobus but kept coming back to it as a safe place to live during school vacations.

The Ruwenberg was more convenient to Den Bos where Meneer v. Mackelenbergh and his family lived. Sometimes on a Sunday they would come and get me, and I would spend a day at their house. Their son Emanuel is my age, and Treesje and Albert were other children with whom I stayed in touch. Two other German kids who were half Jewish, Hans and Klaus Plasterk, were sent to the The Ruwenberg from Eersel. Both are still alive today.

This life went on for about a year, until around 1942. Then the Germans announced that they wanted to use The Ruwenberg as a gijzelaar home. Gijzelaar is the Dutch word for hostage. All the students and everyone had to leave. The Germans then replaced us with young men from the surrounding towns and had them live there, eating and sleeping and doing nothing productive. They were just hostages who were well treated. If anything were to be done against the Germans, in any way, shape, or form, they would take a couple of these hostages and shoot them.

For instance, some of the things that would happen might be an American B-17 would be damaged over Germany and would try to make it back to England. The crew might have to bail out over Holland. The Dutch underground would try to get to the crew and hide them. The nuns in St. Jacobus would hide some of them. If the Germans couldn't find any of the crew, they would shoot some hostages. Or the Dutch underground would go into a town hall and destroy all of the records. Records meant everything. In this country, you can get your birth certificate and know where you were born, that's about it. But over there in those days, they would have everything on you. Your grandparents, your great-grandparents, and so on. They knew who was Jewish and who wasn't, who had a quarter Jewish blood in them. The Dutch underground would try to destroy these things, and again the Germans would kill some hostages. So, to keep all these hostages, we had to leave.

The chaplain of The Ruwenberg had a German name and was a fat, offensive character. I never liked him and was afraid of him. How he ever became a priest I don't know. I was running down the steps, headed to pack my belongings, and he was coming up the steps. Since my name was Levy, even though I was baptized Catholic, everyone knew of course I was Jewish. He asked me, "Are you staying here?"

32

like I was going to be one of the hostages. He was callous, nearly inhuman. I have never forgotten that. My heart went right to my feet, and I was drowning in my own spit. I was already scared to death by everything and then he assumed I would stay as a hostage.

Consequently, back to Eersel and St. Jacobus I went again and things started happening pretty fast. That was the end of my school career for a while. So far, I had had grades one and two in Germany, three, four, and part of five in Holland. Some of the half Jewish kids were also still at St. Jacobus. But the three real Jewish kids there were the same, Ursula, myself, and Ilse Brul.

And then one day they came and got Ilse Brul. One morning they announced that Ilse Brul was going to be taken away, and we all knew it would be to a bad place. There was a car waiting in front of the main entrance for her. The car door was open and a couple policemen were standing there. And I was right there as Ilse Brul came out of the convent door, walked very straight, I remember she had a straight face, pitch black hair, and looked straight ahead, not left or right, walked real erect, and walked into that car. The car drove off and she disappeared, and we never heard from her again. I never will forget that.

Her cousin, Inge Brul, was half Jewish and not taken. She lives even today in Innsbruck, Austria. She confirmed that Ilse died in the camps.

Meneer v. Mackelenbergh thought I'd better go into hiding some place. I don't know whether my sister went into hiding also or not. If so, she was sent to a different place. Once again, I left St. Jacobus and my friends, and went to a really nice town near the border of northern Brabant called Megan. I was right on the River Maas which was a major river, like the Mississippi.

I lived in this home on the River Maas with a housekeeper and four or five young men. These men were in their twenties or early thirties and were workers, construction I believe. I was twelve at the time. It was like a regular house with boarders. I ate breakfast with all of them in the morning, then they would go off to work. All by myself, I'd use a row boat and row up and down the backwater of the river enjoying myself. For lunch, I would come in and eat with all of them and then go out and explore the countryside some more. I would sleep in their rooms at night. There were two men to a room. They never commented on or questioned my presence and always treated me well. I must have been there a couple of months and was very lonely. Then back I came again to St. Jacobus.

Meneer Klaasen was the head of the Dutch police force in Eersel, like the town Chief of Police. He and his family – I knew them – lived on the grounds of the convent in a house that the nuns had provided for them. He would go to mass every day, virtually marching up the aisle in an ostentatiously religious pose, straight to the front. He would wear his boots. He came to me and said he was very sorry, but he had orders from the mayor of the town to take me and my sister to the camps. He apologized, in a perfunctory way, but said he had to do it. He said he would send a couple of policemen to bring us in. He said he would have the policemen dress in plain clothes so that we wouldn't be embarrassed. Only later did I imagine that the plain clothes might have saved him some embarrassment turning over children to Nazis.

The next morning, two policemen did indeed show up and Ursula and I went into a car, just like Ilse Brul. We were carted off to a concentration camp. No one knew that we were under arrest. We stopped at Den Bos and met with Meneer v. Mackelenbergh. I, of course, cried. I didn't want to go to a concentration camp. He said he was very sorry also, and that he would try to get us out. And as it turned out, he had ways to work behind the scenes. So, back we went to the car, and they drove us to the concentration camp, Vught. I went out yet again from St. Jacobus, and it would be a very long time before I came back.

Oh boy, oh boy, we drove in there to the camp. And I got the shock of my life.

Eersel, Holland 2000

The leg of our trip that took us from Cologne, Germany, to Eersel, Holland, involved yet another spine tingling, hair raising autobahn adventure with George and Dan masterfully hanging on during their stints as drivers. The gas pedal was to the floor but there was still the feeling that we might have the little engine that couldn't. The previous night we wanted to see the great cathedral at Cologne, and we were also hungry. Giving in to every worst tourist tendency, we ate at the McDonald's across from the Cathedral. We wanted quick, cheap, and easy, and there it was. And, really, it didn't seem like a normal McDonald's. We enjoyed some McBeer and something called Texas fries that we'd never heard of before (fat French fries). The cathedral was magnificent and held a climate of a thousand years' cold that seeped into our bones.

The routine inside the van had reached a pretty good comfort level. We hauled along certain types of treats carried from home. These included various kinds of granola or breakfast bars along with some fruit that was usually left over from breakfast. Tootsie Roll pops satisfied the sweet tooth. We passed bags and boxes around generously and everyone carried bottled water. George and Dan – or possibly Katie – were normally the front seat passengers. Katie or Dan and Amy and I occupied the center seat, and most often Sue – occasionally relieved by Amy – took the back seat amidst all the luggage. You had to be svelte and limber to ride with the luggage. Rarely did anyone nap in the van. We were either occupied with things to see, things to talk about, things to eat, or stimulated by all the thrills of autobahn riding. Also the distances aren't like cross-country drives in the United States so we never felt we were in for an extremely long haul.

Something needs to the said about the executive officer of the trip, Katie. For months, Katie worked out the plans and all the stops to suit six people and their individual needs and home schedules. She organized the maps, knew how much time we could spare at any one location without a change of itinerary, and made all the reservations for the lot of us. She organized, when necessary, how expenses needed to be split and remained calm and gracious when anyone deviated from the plan.

After decades of being married (not to mention raising five children), this couple was a well-oiled if sometimes noisy machine. Although they could bicker about how to renegotiate the van in a parking spot until it made my eyeballs pop out, this was clearly a communication style they had refined decades ago, and it works for them

If George is 5'6", Katie is 5'3" and slender. Like her husband, she doesn't look her age, 68. She wears jeans well, walks three miles a day at home, has a short, attractive, no-nonsense hairstyle, and, like many registered nurses, a no-nonsense, unsentimental personality (not to be confused with uncaring). If her husband likes to joke and spend money, Katie understands someone has to keep an eye on the prize and make sure important stuff gets done. All the arrangements and amenities for the trip we owed to Katie's efforts.

Although we all loved the hard rolls for breakfast and those neat blanket-comforter things the Germans put on their beds, we were anxious to get back to Holland. George had begun to talk about the good old U.S. of A (as in, "This is pretty but it isn't the good old U.S. of A.") and his understandable malaise among the Germans was catching. An interesting prejudice had developed quickly. We had already decided that the Dutch were friendlier than the Germans, that their language was easier on the ears, that their driving laws were sane, and that they were generally more hospitable. In short, we were making sweeping generalizations left and right and pretty comfortable about it.

When the van rolled across the Dutch border, we all gave a collective sigh. It's not hard to figure out why. We had returned to the land that made some attempt to shelter the young George and left the land that devastated his family and the family of everyone in this van but me. We were headed to Eersel which George to this day considers home.

We noticed right away that the houses of Eersel were, on the whole, smaller and less grand than property we saw in Lippstadt. However, everything was clean and tidy, well maintained. The Dutch cultivated pieces of yard that ordinarily don't seem to exist. For instance, two shared, paved driveways took up almost all of the space between two houses where we visited. However, between one of the driveways and its respective house was about two to three inches of a dirt strip along the whole width of the house. Certainly in the United States it would not be considered a landscaping *faux pas* to ignore this tiny strip. However, the owner of the house had planted tiny flowers all along its length. And this was typical. Every square inch available had something growing on it to beautify.

George noted that the people of Holland pay a much larger share of their income in taxes. Therefore, their houses are modest, they don't ordinarily own vacation homes, or second cars, these kinds of luxuries. But they have much more security in their old age and even younger regarding housing and health maintenance and care. As George put it, "When you're young it probably seems like a bad plan, but when you get a bit older, it makes a lot of sense."

We drove around just getting a feel for the town. Outdoor cafes graced beautiful old streets where folks sat with their coffees and lunches enjoying the ideal weather. Little stores beckoned. We parked. George, with a distinctly proprietary air said, "Nice berg, huh? This used to be a blacksmith shop. We played here all the time when I was little. We'd swear boyhood secret oaths, Sjef Blox and me, on the anvil."

We wandered into what now appeared to be a cross between a hardware store and a Pier 1. Screws and nails and garden hoses were available for purchase as well as trendy looking dishes and furniture. George engaged a young man working at a desk toward the back in conversation. After a minute, George said, "The blacksmith shop is still here! It's through this door." We were invited to proceed and there, over to the side of the old blacksmith shop, stood the very anvil George had mentioned. Now equipment abounded for wood and metal tooling rather than the care of horses, but the place was obviously still in use.

A woman speaking English joined us, the owner and the mother of the young man George had just been talking to. She was the daughter of the previous owner, the one who ran the blacksmith shop when George lived in town so long ago. Again, we were struck by the stability of European family businesses in small towns such as this. The contrast to George's life couldn't have been stronger. George told her that he had been a St. Jacobus kid. She said everyone knew he and his sister were being protected at St. Jacobus – just general knowledge around town. She said, "There are no secrets in a town this small." We told her that we were headed to the house of George's old friend, Sjef Blox. Although Sjef had died a year and a half ago, his widow Jose still lived there, and George and Katie wanted to visit with her.

The Blox house was only a few blocks away. Jose greeted George and Katie with hugs, kisses, and tears upon mentioning Sjef's name. She was still very emotional about his death. No one was speaking English so most of us sat at the dining room table enjoying a cookie and looking around Jose's house.

Like the outside of every house we saw, the inside was equally neat and clean. The old fashioned rotary phone sat on a table, somewhat a relic of the past. Expensive Delft pottery stood atop a large wooden hutch. She had ginger jars, tall and short vases, and salt and pepper shakers of the blue and white pottery. Antique dolls, Dutch boys and girls, kept each other company and watched the visitors in the room with a distant, amused look.

An elaborate chandelier overhung a huge, oval living room coffee table. The cookies on the plate were so neatly arranged, they didn't look real. And pictures of Sjef were placed so that, no matter where we stood or sat, we could see Sjef – and Sjef could see us.

Then, Thea Moors popped in for our visit on a bicycle, the preferred mode of transportation in Eersel and, as far as we could tell, most of Holland. Thea Moors had been a young child care worker at St. Jacobus when George and Ursula were there and went on to become a nun who later ran the operation. She was anxious to show us the new St. Jacobus which now had a different calling. The place had been relocated in the next town over called Duizel and rebuilt as a large home for the retarded. She told us that it was not run by nuns anymore mostly because there weren't so many. She herself had left the order some time ago.

After a while, another person walked into the house, without knocking, we all noted -- the guy from the hardware store. This is truly a small town. He had in hand a book of old American automobiles he was looking to purchase, apparently, and wanted to see if Dan could assist him in some way. They chatted awhile about the cars.

Jose wanted George to go to Sjef's grave with her and, as he put it, "I couldn't refuse." So, Katie, George, and I accompanied Jose to the cemetery behind the Catholic Church in town. "In thankful remembrance to Sjef Blox," the marker said. He had died in 1998. Jose still wept.

Later George talked to us about the strong memories he had of this friendship and the friendship he felt with others in the town. When he came back from the concentration camps to resume school in Eersel, he was so weak, he couldn't ride his bike to school. So Ties and Sjef would ride on either side of him holding hands behind his back and pushing him along. When George first arrived in Eersel, he can recall some boys calling him a "dirty German." But Sjef would stick up for him. "He was a tough kid, a farm kid, and he got into a lot of fights," George commented. His admiration for Sjef's life was so intense that, when he had to give his birth date to the Nazis at the concentration camp, he gave them September 2, Sjef's birthday, because he wanted "to be part of something good."

George's actual birthday is only one day's difference, September 3.

Sjef and Jose had a chance to visit George in Chicago a few years ago. George and Jose laughed about Sjef's reaction to being there. "Sjef Blox in America," George repeated with amazement in a heavy Dutch accent, both arms held out to take in the whole country. "Sjefke Blox in America."

Later, we drove with Thea Moors to Duizel and saw the gallery of pictures showing the history of St. Jacobus at the new facility. There on the wall were pictures of George and Ursula getting ready to leave for Chicago after the war. Also pictured were Ilse Brul, less fortunate, along with Mother Renildus and Thea as a young nun.

George chatted with many people during our brief stay in Eersel and, in contrast to the quiet secretiveness in Lippstadt, he told them all that he had been at St. Jacobus during the war.

That night, after a fruitful shopping trip to a little antique store down the block from the Steensel Hotel, we sat in the hotel bar showing off our new acquisitions. Sue, a pharmacist, had come across some antique apothecary jars which suited her well. I found some hundred year old Delft tiles taken from around the fireplace of an old farmhouse as well as an antique silver frame purchased as a gift for my son.

We were all drinking beer and having a good time enjoying being in Eersel. We continued drinking beer throughout dinner. Finally, it occurred to all of us that Katie was truly relaxing for the first time on this trip. Her good humor and relief that the trip was going so well were infectious. Later, we went for a walk in search of Mother Renildus Lane and encountered what passed for a gang of young teens who were bent on shocking the tourists. They didn't seem so scary after thinking about Nazis for several days. We did find Mother Renildus Lane. Five years ago, George had been given the honor of unveiling the street sign naming the street in honor of the resistance fighting nun. We returned to the hotel to find it full of some sort of business men's conference. Despite our misgivings, everything was quiet that night and we all slept well.

We had all enjoyed our trip to Eersel and it was easy to want to return to a city whose symbol was the "Contented Man." But George's original route back to St. Jacobus and Eersel after being picked up in a Nazi staff car and whisked away, would be a difficult route indeed. The shock of his life, as he put it, took place in Vught.

Part Three -- The Camps:
Vught, Westerbork, and Bergen-Belsen

. . . A covenant with death and an agreement with hell.

(Resolution adopted by the Anti-Slavery
Society, January 27, 1843)

I was in very strange circumstances.

(George Levy Mueller,
Chapter Three)

Vught

It wasn't like going to summer camp. All these SS guys were running around with their guns and high boots. Terrible people. People were getting beat up. They dropped us off and told us to go. I don't remember exactly where they sent me. Ursula says that they separated me from her, that they put me in the men's camp and her in the women's camp. I don't remember that. I remember that we were together all the time from the first night. I was thirteen; Ursula was eight.

The first thing I saw when we were there were all these women running around stark naked. They were newly arrived prisoners. I don't know why they made them do this, but all their clothes were put in a pile. I'm not sure if they gave them prison clothes or if they had to examine their clothes. But they made these women remain naked. This was in April 1943.

So they put me and my sister in these barracks with all women and some children. The women's husbands were in the men's camp. The people that ran this camp were German SS. They also had some local Dutch SS. You know any country, like in the United States, has people who aren't loyal. If Russia had taken over the United States, local communists would have collaborated with them. That's what this is with the Dutch SS. They were regular SS, just Dutch also. The women's camp had women Dutch SS. They had uniforms and were lacking human expression to me, like wax figures. These women were vicious and sadistic. They enjoyed beating up on people.

Three of the SS staff I can explicitly recall are men named Zatoff, Etlinger, and Reineke – all Germans. Zatoff was a sergeant but Etlinger and Reineke were higher, officers. There was also a guy walking around we called the knuppelche which referred to the baton he used to beat people for no reason. He had a great big Colt 45 hanging from his belt, and we never saw him without his bike. He looked unfit for military duty – old, short, and hunchback.

Vught was a concentration camp, and life was very difficult there. If someone violated a rule, this person would be given twenty-five lashes with a horsewhip. All the rest of us would be forced to stand and watch, like at a parade ground. The guard would strap the person down on his stomach on a table or a stretcher and shout, "Einz!" He would bring the horsewhip down on the victim's back. Then, he would scream, "Zwei!" and this would go on for twenty-five times. By the last time, the person's back would look like raw hamburger. Then, he would be carried off.

Now there were also some good parts, if I can call it good parts, in this camp. Before the Nazis converted it, the camp facility existed for other purposes, like a normal recreational type camp. I found a piano in an empty barracks, and I would go play it on my own, and no one would bother me. My sister would listen. We didn't have enough to eat and during the time there, my body began to show the effects of lack of nutrition. The flesh on my thighs caved in as all that remained were bones and muscle. This became my gage for how I was physically doing. I could put my fingers around my ankles. I was thirteen and should have been growing.

During this time, Meneer v. Mackelenbergh concocted a scheme with the Dutch underground in an attempt to save me and Ursula. The plan was to make the Nazis believe that my Uncle Joseph in Chicago was really my father and that somehow things had been mixed up and that they needed to investigate because, in this case, we were not fully Jewish. If we were only half Jewish, the argument went, we shouldn't be in this camp and besides that we would have an American for a father. This meant that their actions toward us would be open to more public, international scrutiny.

Because of this story, the Nazis did start investigating, and they would let Meneer v. Mackelenbergh visit us three or four times in Vught. The German commandant would call for us, and we would find Meneer v. Mackelenbergh waiting. Sometimes he brought his daughter Treesje with him. (We still visit with her.) He looked me over and said, "Yeah, you could be part Aryan. Your eyes are blue. You don't look all that Jewish." He held Ursula gently on his lap in a fatherly way.

The Nazis assigned us a "guardian" named Florence, Flo, another prisoner in the camp. All the other children in the camp were with their mothers, so the idea was that we needed someone to look out for us. One day her name came up on a transport list. If your name was on a transport list, it meant you were being sent to some camp in Poland or Germany, perhaps Bergen-Belsen, Auschwitz, or Dachau. When it was time to go on the trucks, we were standing right there saying good-bye to her, and she started screaming and hollering. The Nazi Etlinger said to me, "Do you need her?"

In a split second, just like it happened yesterday, I remember thinking if I say yes, they might put us on this thing and we'll disappear into thin air, or even if I say no. I didn't know what to say, and I only had a second to think about it. I said, "No." They put her on the truck and until recently I thought she had disappeared. And all these years I thought I had been one of the causes of her death, but I've talked to some learned men about this, and they have told me

I don't have to worry because I was under very strange circumstances. As it turns out, she survived the war and is, to my knowledge, still alive. She lives in Eindhoven, a town in the Netherlands southeast of Den Bos. I wrote her a letter telling her a few things. We had some correspondence. She remembered Ursula and me and told us what camps she was sent to. Most importantly, she didn't blame me for anything.

Since then, I have talked to people, like my old professor and friend, Bernard J. Boelen (a retired professor of philosophy at De Paul University), and they have told me that I should not feel guilty about that because first, I was not grown up. I was only thirteen years old. Second, I was under very trying, very abnormal circumstances. Third, I only had a second to think about it. When I saw the movie "Sophie's Choice," all this came back to me. The character Sophie in the story has only a moment to decide which child to give up to the Nazis for certain death knowing that if she refuses to choose, both children will die. The decision haunts her the rest of her life. I've been told this is a "choiceless choice," but, even knowing Florence survived, this is a difficult experience to look back on.

Meneer v. Mackelenbergh had worked with the camp commandant to allow Ursula and me to visit him outside the camp, at his house, during a Dutch national holiday in late fall or early winter. He, in fact, planned not to return us to the camp. I don't know the details of this plan. Perhaps he was going to hide us somewhere and say we ran away or perhaps he thought he could talk the Germans into letting us out since we were presumably only half Jewish.

However, the Germans had a change of command. Our camp commandant was removed, ordered back to Germany, and a new one took his place. Quickly, he had our names on a transport list. Despite Meneer v. Mackelenbergh's argument that he shouldn't do that, that they had our identity wrong, he said, "I don't care. They are here, and they're going."

One of the saddest parts of Vught was the way families were parted. Whenever they had a transport listed, they would announce that these particular people would be sent tomorrow on the trucks or the trains to some other camp someplace, many to Westerbork first. They would announce the names, and then they would bring the husbands over from the separate men's section. The Nazis would say, "You have ten minutes to say good-bye." These husbands and wives, with the children that were there with the mother, had only ten minutes to spend together. They would hug, kiss, and cry – terrible wailing. I saw this happen many times.

To me that was one of the worst things in the whole camp, worse even than the beatings and whippings. They would have maybe one hundred people all standing in this big, open place like a playground. And we would be right there near them. They were crying, and they knew they would never see each other again. They would say, "We'll see you again," but deep down, they knew better. Or maybe they didn't. But that's how it seemed to me. That was such a sad thing, one of the worst parts of this whole Holocaust story.

Since the nuns had told me that my mother had died before I left St. Jacobus, I knew we had no parents. I remember thinking that I was glad, if you can imagine. I am serious about this. I was glad that I didn't have any parents, that we didn't have to go through this.

So, we were put on a transport list to a new camp, Westerbork, in Northern Holland. In October 1943, we were put on trucks, the trucks went to the train, and the train went to Westerbork.

Westerbork

Now Westerbork was a better camp. Vught was supposed to be a transit camp but was administered like the most vicious concentration camp. Westerbork was a transit camp where the administrative purpose was to simply hold people until they could be sent on. Of course, they were sent on more often than not to Auschwitz, but I'm thinking now about the conditions of living in the camp itself. Jews from all over Holland came through Westerbork. The major concentration camps in Germany, Lithuania, and Poland received prisoners from Westerbork including Sobibor which is infamous for having only nineteen Jews received from Westerbork survive out of more than 34,000.

Part of the reason for the improved conditions at Westerbork as opposed to Vught was that the German SS had little to do with the lower level operations of the camp, dealing with conditions and prisoners. The camp was guarded by the Dutch police who were not mean. They were strictly there to make sure we didn't run away.

One of the first things that happened when we arrived at Westerbork was an outbreak of polio. As soon as we got there, we were assigned to the quarantined barracks that had the polio outbreak. So, we were confined to barracks and, although the length of time was only probably a week or two, it seemed like an eternity. After the quarantine was lifted, we could wander around the camp.

At this point, I felt, rather suddenly, very religious. I think it was a sort of "foxhole" reaction, this religious feeling, and I was surrounded by people practicing Judaism. I missed St. Jacobus and my friends like Sjef. But they had a few Catholics there and someone I believe was a priest. I received communion secretly.

The Jewish people set up some semblance of society in the camp. They made sure the kids were learning something through a sort of haphazard school system. And they had some kind of a government among the Jewish prisoners. We couldn't just run wild.

We were there around four months. Then, one day our names came up, Ursula's and mine, on the transport list dated February 15, 1944, and we were sent to Belsen, Germany, an overnight trip, on that same day. I remember being on this train, and we stopped in different railroad stations. I can distinctly remember a train slowing, going the opposite way from us. I could see the people, and I remember thinking, "Boy, do I wish I was one of those

47

people!" They could get off at the next stop or where ever they wanted, but I was a prisoner on that train going somewhere that I didn't want to go. Then, we arrived in Belsen near the town of Bergen and near Hanover, Germany. We had no idea what awaited us here or how long we would be here.

Bergen-Belsen

The camp at Bergen-Belsen, located between the two small towns, seemed very big, like a complete town with streets and different sections. We were driven in trucks to a compound within the larger camp where we remained until leaving Bergen-Belsen.

The Germans had a separate compound for every category of people. So, there would be a section for German Jews, a section for Dutch Jews, a section for Russian prisoners, and so on. Ursula and I were placed in the section for Dutch Jews. As odd as it may sound, we were in a "preferred" place, I guess you'd say. By this, I mean that the people in this location were somehow categorized as not on their way to the death camps at that point. The reasons were various. In our case, my Uncle Joseph's plan to cast doubt on our true identify as well as identify us with America put us in this category. We might, in the right circumstances, be worth a trade. Or the Germans might feel they'd have more of a public relations problem getting rid of this group of people. The thinking now is that some combination along these lines kept us in this category.

Although it was very unusual, I was able to keep my sister with me in the men's barracks. Picture the barracks as being very crowded with beds close together and stacked three high. The space between the bunks was narrow but enough room to walk. The beds themselves were stacked too close together to allow for sitting up in them. Wooden planks formed slats which supported the straw mattresses.

In the summertime, the barracks heated up to where we could hardly stand it. Very early, maybe 4:00 – 5:00 a.m., they would get everybody out of bed, and we'd stand outside to be counted which was called appel, roll call. This would take a long time, sometimes hours. We'd have to stand there for the count. The Nazis had a number in mind for how many there should be, but of course it rarely worked out at first. The numbers were always off, so the count would begin again. People would fall over and die in the heat.

Able adults were sent to work after receiving hot soup or hot coffee which was more like black water. The Germans had factories there and used forced labor from the camp's inmates. They worked until they were exhausted and beyond. Guards beat them for lagging behind or any reason. Kids like me were left alone. I must say, we didn't have to work but just hung around. I did make some friends with other kids. In the beginning, we were in fairly good, healthy shape. So, we played games and actually had races among ourselves. We were kids playing kids' games.

At the end of the barracks there were a couple of sinks where we could wash. We had an outdoor toilet which was in horrible condition. Furthermore, Ursula and I shared the same bunk bed sleeping at opposite ends. As time went on, this camp and its conditions got worse and worse. Then winter came and there was no heat. This was a climate with cold and snow. People would steal the planks from each other's beds to make fires. In the end, we'd have two end planks and only one center one to support the straw mattress. I still have a scar on my hip from sleeping on this wood with open sores.

Also, everything was very filthy. Everyone had diarrhea. People tried to go to the bathroom in the filthy, horrible outdoor bathroom. But then mostly at some point people just went right where they stood.

During the "good" times, we received no more than 700 – 800 calories of food each day. Soup had chunks of horse meat in it, but very little. Mostly, it had turnips.

The nightmare roll call situation became increasingly worse in the cold weather and as everyone became weaker. Often, we would have to stand for appel for hours in the cold and snow, and we were weak and had little in the way of clothes on, maybe an old pair of shoes and maybe a little coat or something. Now I get cold if it is freezing outside and I have my down jacket. How I stood there like that I don't know, but we stood for hours and hours.

The German SS would come count us. They were assisted by people called kapos who were also prisoners. For instance, when Germany over-ran Poland and Russia, they took prisoners, sometimes out of the Polish or Russian prisons. These were murderers and criminals. The Nazis would tell them, "Listen, you can either rot in this prison or you can get a nice job as a foreman in a concentration camp." Although they were still prisoners, they were well-fed and strong. The two main kapos we called Casimir de Groote ("Cashmere the Big") and Casimir de Klijne ("Cashmere the Small"). They had green triangles on their chests. Everyone had their designation. Red for instance meant political prisoners, such as captured members of the Dutch underground. Of course, we had the yellow Star of David.

The kapos would do the actual counting. These guys were as bad or worse than the SS. I remember once we were all standing out there being counted, and it was cold and somebody had remained back in the barracks because he was sick. So, they dragged him out and made him stand right next to me. This man was really skinny and weak and a kapo beat him until he was on the ground and then kicked him and kicked him. Finally, the SS man with him couldn't even take it any more and told him to stop. The man died right after that. Conditions were horrible.

People became somewhat crazed under these conditions also. We always had to stand in the same formation. One man, who was a doctor, would constantly talk about calories while we were standing there waiting while the other sections were being counted. Calories, calories, we don't get enough calories; he'd go on and on.

Thousands and thousands of prisoners were counted this way each morning. The kapos would report the count to the SS man who would report it to a higher SS man and so on. Although they were afraid of someone having escaped when the numbers were off, the place was well guarded with guard towers with machine guns pointed right at us. I don't see how anyone could have escaped from there. In addition to the guards and guard towers, we were surrounded by electrified barbed wire and dogs patrolling.

One of the things I loved were the American B-17's and B-24's that would come over during the day. The skies were black with them. We could tell from the direction they were flying what cities they were going to bomb. When they hit Hanover, we could hear the bombs falling. It was music to our ears. At night, it would be the British, the Lancasters coming over. One time there was a dog fight of German planes and P-38's. A P-38 was shooting at the camp it seemed. Perhaps they were trying to hit the army base nearby. The German plane was shot down. The guards in the towers were shooting at the P-38's. I was standing out there watching and a big shell casing, like a fifty caliber machine gun casing, came tumbling out of the sky and landed right by my feet. The barracks we were staying in were shot up, either by the guards or the planes, I don't know, but one man was killed as I recall. He sat up in his bunk, and a bullet ripped through the place and right through his stomach. This was the winter of 1944. Times were getting worse, and Germany was losing the war. The next day after these air attacks the guards would be even more vicious, maybe because of anger over their own losses.

Once a week we were taken to the showers. We'd take off our clothes, take our shower, then put our clothes right back on. Putting the clothes right back on was a horrible experience because they were full of lice. Thousands of lice were all over my clothes and my body. It took an hour after the shower for the lice to sort of settle down again. Everyone had them. I used to spend my spare time killing the lice between my thumbs. They would pop and spatter up, sometimes hitting my face. The linings of my clothes were solid with lice eggs.

During this time in Bergen-Belsen, I apparently came down with hepatitis. We had no mirrors, but people told me my face and eyes were yellow. Also, my urine was orange-brown. I was sick for a while and still had to stand for apel, but I recovered without medicine or drugs which were unavailable to us.

As conditions worsened, so did the food. Pretty soon all we had to eat was the equivalent of two slices of bread every three days with a little pat of butter, a little margarine or jam. Then we had the hot watery soup with turnips every day and the hot water for what they called coffee. That's it; maybe a couple hundred calories per day, if we want to talk calories. I would get the food for Ursula and me, and I would take both of our rations of food and divide it between us. For instance, I would divide our piece of bread. I would always cut myself a tiny bit more, not a lot, but like if you cut it in half, I would take the bigger half. For years, I felt guilty about that. But I rationalized it at the time saying that I was bigger and needed more to eat, and that I needed to be there to take care of my sister. Again, I talked to some learned people who told me there is nothing to feel guilty about.

I also took care of my sister, if I may say so myself. I combed her hair and kept her with me, things like that. One time on the way home from the showers, we walked past a pile of potatoes, and I grabbed a couple and put them in my pockets. The SS guard saw me, and he came and said something to me as we were marching back to the barracks. I thought he was going to kill me or shoot me; I didn't know what he was going to do. He just made me throw the potatoes back and then let me go.

By this time, I was very skinny and weak. My legs were not swollen at the bottom like those about to die but that is because I was young and because I was well nourished from my parents and then later the nuns. However, my legs would swell when I would put my feet down on the floor and sit. During this sitting position, fluid would go to my ankles. But the minute I put my feet up, the swelling would go away.

Like everyone else, I also had constant diarrhea. I had diarrhea for at least a year, possibly two. Dysentery. Although I could walk, I was so weak that I could not run without falling down. As a fourteen year old, I wanted to run but as soon as I tried it, I would fall on my face. My knees would just give out. I was that weak. That's the condition I was in.

We were also issued cigarettes each week, I don't know why. It shows you the power of the smoking addiction. There were two people there, Izzy and his son. Izzy would trade his piece of bread for my sister's and my cigarettes. He wouldn't have anything to eat. I said, "Izzy, you will die," but he said he had to have a cigarette. And he died.

But dying was no big deal. Everybody died. Let me explain about this dying thing. There was a man walking around with great big ankles. His ankles were the size of his knees. What I later learned from Uncle Joseph is that the lack of protein caused the osmotic balance in the body to lose the fluids from the tissues which all settled on the bottom of the legs. People in this condition would shuffle around, and we could tell that they would be dead within one or two hours. Lots of people were like this. They were all skin and bones, just shuffling along. Many times during the day they would cry, "Ahhhhhh," and then just fall out and die or pass out. It didn't make any difference. If you looked like you were dead, you were dead. We would then go over and grab this person's clothes if he had better ones. After taking his clothes, we would line him up against the barracks with his head against the barracks and his feet extended toward the sidewalk. After awhile, the whole barracks, one side to the other, would be full of dead bodies. Then, once or twice a week, on the main street, right outside our compound, there would come this big wagon that was originally meant to be pulled by horses. But prisoners pushed and pulled it. They had already been to other compounds. It was like the garbage truck going around your neighborhoods. They would come into ours and four prisoners would grab these bodies and carry them out to this big wagon tossing the bodies up onto it. The bodies would be piled like a hay stack, thrown up there like bags of sand or potatoes. Just like collecting the garbage. Then they went on to the next compound.

Two men were living in a tiny little barracks just big enough for two, like a small Quonset hut, situated across the road. I could see them, two Jewish guys, and they appeared to be in good shape. They were given enough to eat and were clearly living better than the rest of us. I always envied them in a way because they slept good and they ate good, but they worked in a place where they had all these dead bodies.

What they did with these bodies is not clear. Rumors were they knocked teeth out or cut out hair. And some of the bodies were sent to an on-site crematorium, not a huge one but one intended to get rid of the dead. The story goes that these two guys knew too much of what was going on regarding the dead, even more than we knew. So they were treated better, but if the war came to an end, the Germans would kill them right away. In other words, they were for sure going to die because they knew too much. I don't know what happened to them after the war.

Although I was fourteen years old, sex or adolescent sex drive was no factor in camp life. I only had an interest in two things, food and freedom. One hundred percent of the talk at the camp was about food or getting out, nothing else. Food was absolutely paramount. One night, I got the food for my sister and myself, and we were sitting in our bed eating. We were in a half crouch in the middle bunk. A man was below us and another one above. The man on top of us had a bucket strung to the guy on the top of the next bunk over. Both these men would urinate and defecate in this bucket.

Ursula and I were just eating our rations and one of the men dumped the bucket by mistake causing it to fall on our bed, on the food and everything. This whole bucket dumped all over our bunk and food, and we still ate. Now that's enough to make you sick, but this is a true story. Those were the conditions we were in. The smell had to be terrible but we were used to it and couldn't smell it. Later, I talked to a doctor in the American Army who was one of the first people into the camp. He said he could smell it ten miles out, that the smell alone made him sick.

I don't have much good to say about the whole stay in Bergen-Belsen, but there was one act of kindness that I remember. A neighboring compound held Jewish men who were sent in from Auschwitz. They were all men and looked in terrible condition. We were not allowed to talk to them. Barbed wire guarded their compound from ours. But at night some of the men from our compound and women from the women's barracks would go to the barbed wire and talk to these men trying to hear news of family and loved ones, wives and husbands. In the dark, they would talk to one of these men and say, "Have you seen my husband? He's from Amsterdam and he was sent to Auschwitz from Westerbork," for instance. And the reply might be, "Well, maybe come back tomorrow because my friend, so and so, knew somebody by the name of Bloomenfeld that could have been your husband." And so people would talk back and forth like that and find out news. The men would tell them, "I've seen your husband and he's alive," or "He's dead." That's the kind of contact we had. These men were in terrible condition. They all had tattoos from being in Auschwitz.

So, one night I went toward this men's compound on my own. It was pitch dark, and I don't really remember why I was going there. An SS guard with a gun stopped me. He was not in the tower but just walking, and said, "What do you want?" I said, "I am so hungry I can't take it anymore." I have, by this point, been eating wood, for instance – anything to lessen the hunger pangs. I said, "I have a little sister who is with me." Maybe I played on his sympathy. I said, "I am so hungry. I must have something to eat." The SS guard looked like he was in his early twenties. He said to me, "Come back tomorrow, and I will give you a piece of bread. I don't have anything now." This was toward the end of the war, and the Germans didn't have any food themselves to speak of. I told nobody about this. The next night, I went there in the pitch dark, and I said I was the guy from last night. "Do you remember me?" He said, "Here." He gave me a piece of bread. I said, "Thank you." That was all there was to it. I returned and gave my sister half and I ate half. I want to say that there are some people in this world that are not all bad.

Also, I did the same thing with the head kapo. I went to the main kapo, the head of all of the kapos in this compound that we were in, Walter Hanke, a murderer. I said I wanted to see him. He was not the guy, not the kapo that was beating people, but he was in charge. I went to him and I said, "I have to have something to eat, and I have a little sister." He gave me a piece of bread, too, and didn't kill me. So, not everybody was one hundred percent bad. People just can't understand the conditions. If I talked for hours, people wouldn't really understand the conditions.

I need to mention two people I met in Bergen-Belsen. Wherever we were, even in Hyplaat in Holland, in the beginning, and then Westerbork, the Jewish people organized, made sure the children, for instance, learned something. Anyway, I met two people in Bergen-Belsen, two elderly men who were very different. One of them had a violin. I don't know how he got this violin. He played it so beautifully. Another man I met had a long beard and was a very smart man. There's a card trick where you put eleven cards in three rows and you say, "Pick a row." Your card is in that row and then you put that row in the middle and you do that three times, then count the eleventh card, and that's your card. Anyway, this man explained to me the mathematics behind this. He sat and talked to me, and I think that's amazing that he tried to explain it to me. Of course, I didn't understand. I recall he was quite an old man.

Since I was baptized a Catholic, the Orthodox Jews didn't think that I was really Jewish. They said I was a Catholic, not a Jew. So, I don't know what I am. But on Friday nights, they would pray using the back part of the barracks, a filthy place with one light bulb hanging down. They would ask me to be the Shabbes Goy, the Sabbath Gentile. It was a sin for them to turn the light on or off or to do any type of work, so they would ask me to turn the light on for them. I was also expected to sweep the floor to try to get the excrement off so that they could have some semblance of prayer. Even at that early age, I was questioning religion, under those conditions. I remember asking one of them, "If it's a sin to turn the light on for you, how come it's not a sin for me? Either it's wrong or it isn't wrong. You are asking me to do something that you consider wrong." I remember asking him that. The answer he gave me was that it was only wrong for Jews, and since I wasn't a real Jew anymore, I could go ahead and do it. I have never forgotten that. I feel that way about religion now. It's either wrong or it isn't wrong, and God doesn't care if you turn the light on or not. It's wrong to kill somebody, for anybody. That's the way I believe.

I'll mention one other couple whom I met at Bergen-Belsen, Dr. And Mrs. Melkman who had, I believe, a little boy with them. And they befriended us. Dr. Melkman was a very nice man, probably in his thirties. They were prisoners, just like we were, and they had this child with them. Dr. Melkman was staying in the men's barracks, but he would spend his free time with his wife and son. They kind of adopted Ursula and me, and we shared things with them, social things if you can say something like that. We knew where they would live after the war and kept in touch. In 1947 on the eve of coming to the United States, Ursula and I were in Amsterdam preparing for our flight. We said, "Let's see if we can find the Melkmans." Sure enough, we found them living in Amsterdam. They had a house, and he was once again a professor at a university in Amsterdam. I then noticed a little son. This wasn't the same little son that they had in Bergen-Belsen.

So, they told me the story, that when they were living in Amsterdam before the Germans took them prisoner, they had a little son. In the middle of the night, the Germans came and took all these people and grabbed them out of their homes and sent them to Westerbork. In the confusion, their son ended up with another couple and this other couple's son ended up with the Melkmans. They never said anything about this when we were back in Bergen-Belsen. They were afraid to say anything for fear that the Nazis would take away this boy. So, they told no one, not even us. The good part of this story is that the Melkmans and both children survived the war.

But back to being in Bergen-Belsen. In January or February 1945, I knew that I was going to get out of there before too long. The weather was getting warmer, winter not quite so cold. Every once in a while I still think about that. I could stand up against one of those buildings in the barracks in the sun, and it would be warm. And the war was coming closer and closer to an end. Everyone knew that. Then one day they announced that we were going somewhere. Not everybody, but a bunch of people, and our names were on the list. They told us to get our belongings, whatever we had.

I had little more than the clothes on my back. I also had my spoon that I carried with me wherever I went which was very important. Whenever I saw any type of food or any kind of pot, I would dig into it and eat. Sometimes my life seems surreal when I sit at home or in our cottage in the north woods, drinking wine, smoking a cigar from Key West, eating cheese, and thinking about those days.

After we gathered our belongings, we left the compound and gathered along the main road where others had assembled from their compounds. Despite the many rumors, no one knew where we were going, but 2500 of us were put on a train out of Bergen-Belsen.

58

Bergen-Belsen 2000

The six of us had spent the night in the small German town of Celle, near Bergen-Belsen. Celle, much more than Lippstadt, seems like a tourist town. The old, quaint town has buildings of the typical stucco with red tiled roofs. Many shops and restaurants give visitors opportunities to spend their Deutschmarks. The previous night, we'd found a good restaurant and several of us tried the sauerkraut, feeling like we should do this once while in Germany. We drank a little local beer with our meal and enjoyed looking in shop windows. Because we had arrived on Sunday, the shops were closed until the next day. Sue found what she felt were some perfect wine glasses for a gift for a friend back home and hoped to get back to the store the next morning to buy them, but we never found the time.

Earlier that day, we had arrived at the museum and grounds at Bergen-Belsen and decided that we could look around at the exhibits on the grounds and maybe in the museum still that afternoon. The next morning, we had an appointment with Thomas Rahe, an historian and the curator of the Bergen-Belsen museum and memorial. So, we followed the paths as they wound around the grounds.

The experience of visiting the grounds at Bergen-Belsen is not unlike visiting Civil War battle sites in the United States. Even though the virtual city that George described was comprised of extensive buildings at the concentration camp, they had all been burned to the ground by the British to prevent the spread of typhus after the camp was liberated. No original structures remain. What does remain are mass graves with collective markers such as, "Here lie 3,000 dead." Quite a few, as George remarked. There are a number of these all around the grounds with different figures, always in the thousands. The graves were visible as mounds rolling across the flat countryside of the grounds. As the museum film informed us, thousands of bodies were literally bulldozed into mass graves under the supervision of the British Army. The number of dead was so overwhelming that nothing else was possible especially with the concern of the spread of disease. Nazis were forced on the bulldozers and other machinery to perform the unpleasant task of cleaning up after themselves as British photographers took the pictures that to this day remain among the most graphic coming out of World War II and the Holocaust.

Another striking feature of the camp grounds is its loneliness. Even though the towns of Bergen and Belsen aren't too far, these are very small towns and the camp grounds are located in heavily wooded countryside. One could only imagine how the prisoners felt after being transported two hundred miles from Westerbork to this place in the middle of nowhere except the Third Reich. A huge military installation is nearby as it was during World War II when it was home to a Panzer division. What might be viewed as a location of peaceful, sylvan beauty only took on the impression of sinister isolation, almost Gothic in its proportions, in the context of our visit.

Some say such places have an almost haunted feel to them, but it felt more like we were the ghosts floating over the reality of the events long past. We kept our jackets zipped against the cool spring air accompanied by only a few other visitors. To George, this location conjured up concrete, not abstract memories, and he momentarily and uncharacteristically shed some tears.

As we piled back into the minivan, George remarked, not for the first time, "I'm tired of this. This is it. I'm not coming back here for this anymore. Next time I come to Europe, it will be for a real vacation." We all slumped quietly in our seats, and I really wondered if this project were worth the cost.

The next morning, we pulled into the parking lot of the museum just at 9:00 a.m., in time for our appointment with Dr. Thomas Rahe who pulled in right behind us. He greeted George immediately, and we were all introduced. This trip provided constant paradoxes for all of us. The negative feeling toward the German population was contrasted with the close friendship with Hans Boenicke, and now it was once again challenged by the distinguished, intelligent presence of Thomas Rahe. His fluent English has an almost British, James Bond quality to it which he told us he's heard before, yet he never studied in England. He is a German non-Jew who specialized in his studies in German Jewish history. His job search came serendipitously at the time when a search was conducted for a new curator at the Bergen-Belsen museum and memorial.

He directed us into a small library with a conference table that we all gathered around. Without notes and with complete comfort and interest in talking to George, Dr. Rahe gave us more than two hours of his time. George had several questions for him which Dr. Rahe responded to knowledgeably. For starters, George wanted to confirm the location of Anne Frank's barracks as opposed to his own. Dr. Rahe pulled out a map of the reconstructed camp pointing to the Sternlager – Star Camp (so-called because of the Star of David worn by each prisoner in this sector) – section that George lived in. He pointed out a small women's barracks built rather late in the war. This is where Anne Frank lived out her final days before dying of some combination of starvation and disease.

George was also curious about the two men living in the Quonset hut that he had told us about, the ones who were prisoners but were in charge of doing something regarding the bodies. Dr. Rahe said that these men actually kept a diary which was recovered after the war. They are assumed to have died before the war's end, but this text, currently unpublished, could be made available. They were around the age of twenty-four.

George asked about the head kapo who gave him the piece of bread, as related previously. Dr. Rahe said that this guard was really one of the men pulled out of German prisons. In this case, he had been serving time for murder, but other accounts also suggest that he was capable of periodic acts of kindness. Two things are striking about this story: One, that garden variety murderers weren't as bad as law abiding Nazis, and two, that more than fifty years later, George placed such importance on the kindness of giving him this single piece of bread. What strange circumstances indeed to lead one to be so grateful for such a small act of kindness in the face of such great acts of atrocity.

Dr. Rahe discussed the Jewish block leaders who held court and had the authority to imprison, within the larger prison, other inmates violating acceptable codes of behavior such as stealing food. George commented, "I stole bread. I just never got caught." Dr. Rahe said that it was a question, "What to do when children stole bread? In the face of such great hunger, it was understandable."

George has a memory, not very detailed, of being assigned some work in a hospital within the camp and wondered if that were possible. Dr. Rahe said, "Yes, it is possible. There were two hospitals in the camp." He went on to say that it has been impossible to accurately locate the hospitals in their reconstructed model of the premises.

Dr. Rahe explained the special nature of the Bergen-Belsen prisoners, at least at the beginning. The prisoners really were seen as possible exchange prisoners and held for this purpose. There was never an expectation of killing them. So, the prisoners were allowed certain "privileges" such as wearing civilian clothes and bringing in luggage, if they had anything, with them. They didn't receive tattoos like Auschwitz, for example. Since many Germans lived in, for instance, Great Britain and the United States, but not so many U.S. or British citizens lived in Germany, holding Jews with ostensible connections seemed necessary to this way of thinking. Thus, one might be assigned to Bergen-Belsen by virtue of dual citizenship, a Palestine certificate, or another connection like George and Ursula with their Uncle Joseph in Chicago. That's why conditions in the camp were on the better side at the beginning and why some drawings exist made by Jewish prisoners. They were able to bring in paper, pen, pencils, paints.

These conditions changed in 1944 and actually the conditions of Bergen-Belsen ended up worse than the death camps where one might expect to live if one could only avoid selection. But it was, Dr. Rahe said, "Incalculable what would happen to you," in Bergen-Belsen. Beginning in March of 1945, he told us, 18,000 people died in four weeks.

Toward the end of the war, the Nazis began emptying out the death camps such as Auschwitz and Dachau, because they wanted none of these prisoners found alive there. So, they either shot them or transported them out. One of the destinations was Bergen-Belsen which explains the influx of thousands of prisoners that did not "fit the concept," as Dr. Rahe put it, of the exchange prisoners. At the end of the war, there were still 700,000 concentration camp inmates living. Bergen-Belsen's location at the center of the Reich was, the Germans thought, protected as much as possible, and they were not realistic about their chances of winning the war at some point.

By February and March of 1945, the Nazis had way too many bodies to know what to do with at Bergen-Belsen. People were dying in huge numbers due to starvation and typhus. Dr. Rahe told of the Nazi plan to burn the bodies outside in fields. But these fires would burn into the night and the huge, nearby military installation complained through their commandant that this must stop because it is a real military danger. The Royal Air Force and United States Air Force used the fires of the burning bodies to bomb the military installation. The irony was lost on no one that the final use of these Jewish bodies would be to illuminate targets for the Allied bombers. So, this method of disposal "did not function," according to Dr. Rahe.

This eventually led, of course, to the horrendous documentation that still shocks when the camp was liberated by the British. All these dead bodies and starving, disease ridden prisoners were captured on film for the world to see, exactly what the Third Reich had wanted to avoid.

George and Thomas Rahe still had a few people and events to discuss. George commented on v. Mackelenbergh and his uncle's plot to confuse the Nazis about their identity. Dr. Rahe characterized this as an effective and intelligent kind of resistance. He gave another example of resistance under circumstances where it appeared that the person was powerless. Mrs. Birnbaum was a prisoner at Westerbork in charge of a number of orphans. She went to the camp commandant demanding to know why so many non-Jewish children were interned at the camp. Non-Jewish? Wondered the commandant. Yes, I know what Jews look like, countered Mrs. Birnbaum. She cast doubt with these very young orphans who were too young to tell their names. According to Dr. Rahe, this played cleverly on the German desire to justify their murders and if the justification had to do with Jewishness, then this had to be straightened out. So, the children were sent to Bergen-Belsen instead of Auschwitz, along with Mrs. Birnbaum, and many of them survived the war. Power among the powerless, an intelligent and effective resistance.

George said he didn't know Mrs. Birnbaum, that he was on his own except for Mr. Melkman. Dr. Rahe knew the Melkmans and knew that Mr. Melkman is still alive. He also pointed out how important the survivor accounts are because the child with the Melkmans, not the Melkman's child, would not have been properly accounted for in the historical record. "The lists lie in this respect," commented Dr. Rahe.

Dr. Rahe went on to talk about the use of survivor accounts and the fact that some very conservative historians dismiss them. "Historians are trained to look at the files," he said which are assumed to be objective documentation. But, he went on, this is more a matter of not knowing how to interpret the information gained from survivor stories. "The problem is not in the account, but in the historian," and his ability to ask the right questions of the account.

An intriguing example he gave was of an account by a gypsy who was a small child in Bergen-Belsen. She related a memory of Commandant Kramer coming to her barracks and seeing how the children were starving. He said, "This won't do. We can't have these children starving," and made soup and fed the children himself. Then things returned to normal. "Do I believe that Kramer personally cooked soup for the children because they were so hungry? Of course not. It's ludicrous. But it does tell us how a young child psychologically copes with the fear of death by starvation. When I started here, I would have put this aside. In the meantime, I have changed my mind. You must be interdisciplinary always. You wouldn't be a good historian here if you were only a historian."

Dr. Rahe also discussed what the group perceived as an almost "sudden" interest in Holocaust history within the past ten years. Dr. Rahe dismissed the idea that Spielberg caused it by his movie "Schindler's List," but rather thinks the movie was an outgrowth of the increasing audience and interest. In the 1950's and into the 60's, no one could get their accounts published. No one, not even in Israel, wanted to hear. Speakers trying to communicate the conditions in the camp would be met by statements such as, "Oh, yes, it was very difficult even in America. For years we had no sugar." Survivors understood that people didn't want to understand.

In 1966, a little museum existed at Bergen-Belsen consisting primarily of photographs taken by the British upon liberation of the camp. There had been absolutely no archives, no collecting, and no contact with survivors. Dr. Rahe, from 1987 – 1990, "started from scratch in many respects. There are some things in life you can't correct and this is one of them. Everyone now was relatively young at the time of liberation." But their stories are forming a more complete archive which we were surrounded by in the room.

German Jewish history is still a highly sensitive topic, Dr. Rahe said. There is still this thing in Germany, "Oh, what words do you use when you speak with Jews? Do not say anything wrong!" Dr. Rahe elaborated, "It's hard to imagine what atmosphere comes from speaking the word 'Juden' here in Germany. It has so much connotation, so much psychological intensity. More than 'nigger' in the United States. It is emotionally and psychologically complicated. There is no question of normalcy. Someone saying, 'I'm Jewish,' changes the atmosphere in the room totally. It's a very important piece of information. Only in the last twenty years have historians taken an interest in German Jews and almost all the work is by non-Jews."

One example Dr. Rahe gave was a survey done in numerous German communities, such as Lippstadt. The question was asked, "How many Jews are living here?" In the case of Lippstadt, a town of 250,000 inhabitants, the answers ranged from 8,000 – 125,000. The true number: 120. And this repeats itself over and over and over, according to Thomas Rahe. "A group about which so much is spoken, there must be a lot of." The overall perception: "too many Jews," says Dr. Rahe. (Hans Boenicke is obviously an exception, perceiving that Jews have almost totally disappeared from Lippstadt. But perhaps it's just all the Jews that he knew growing up.)

We had learned considerable from our talk with Dr. Rahe.

Part Four – Train to Nowhere, Train to Freedom

It is easy to go down into hell; night and day the gates of dark death stand wide; but to climb back again, to retrace one's steps to the open air – there's the rub, the task.

(Virgil, The Aeneid)

The train that George and Ursula were put on is generally known as The Lost Transport which pulled out of Bergen-Belsen April 10, 1945, only five days ahead of the British Army liberating the camp. Although the train ended up in Trobitz, this is not its likely destination. As Thomas Rahe continued to talk to us, he and George discussed this train. Rahe noted that only those prisoners who were defined as possible exchange prisoners were placed on the train. This leads historians to believe that the Nazis still imagined a use for these prisoners even this late in the war, virtually on the eve of defeat.

We left the museum. George, who only a few hours before had declared that he'd never come back, said, "I'll come back and see Dr. Rahe." Indeed, Thomas Rahe's way of discussing an incredible range of issues with survivors and families without drama or self-consciousness or condescension, is remarkable.

We drove freely away from the camp site in our minivan. But in 1945, although George and Ursula left the camp, they were not yet free.

*** 1945 ***

All these people, mostly from our compound, the Star Camp, were taken to the railway stop. We didn't know where we were going but there were plenty of rumors. Some thought we were going to Theresienstadt, a so-called model camp near Prague. Or perhaps we were going somewhere to be killed. Or maybe they were going to blow up a bridge and the train and all of us with it. No one really knew. But mostly we hoped we were going to a better place.

A few men, three or four, got out of their compound somehow and managed to mingle with us. They wanted to come with us on the train. They were from the group of men who had been brought in late in the war from Auschwitz. Izzy's son was there – Izzy who had traded away food for cigarettes and died. Izzy's son informed to the SS on the men who mingled with us. No one of us was going to identify them, but since they had been in Auschwitz, it only took the Nazis a few minutes to check arms and find those with the tattoos like they gave prisoners in Auschwitz. They then beat the living daylights out of them kicking them under the rolls of barbed wire back toward their compound. After they got through the barbed wire and back to their compound, they were a bloody, raw mess. What's so amazing is that nothing bothered me. I could just stand there and look at it, and it was just another thing to see.

The train was so crowded by the time they loaded 2500 passengers aboard, many had to stand including us. Some of the cars were like cattle cars and some passenger cars. The train wound east. The progress was very slow. The train was avoiding the Allies closing in from the west and the Russians closing in from the east, but we really didn't know that at the time. However, we did know the Allies were bombing everyday. So we rode just a few miles a day, and then we stopped while they repaired track ahead, for instance.

Conditions on the train were terrible. We didn't have food and had to scavenge for it, and water wasn't given to us in the cars. When we stopped, I would go up to the engine and ask for some of the hot water. The engineer would tell me to hold my pan out and then would release some hot water into it. And people were dying every day. I had befriended one lady in Bergen-Belsen who was Catholic like me. I felt a kinship with her. Every day when the train stopped, I walked over to the box car where she was riding and visited with her. One time I was looking for her after the train stopped, and I couldn't find her. Someone said, "She's laying over there." She was dead with the rest of the people laying there.

I could have escaped from this train very easily. As a matter of fact, when the train stopped, we would get out and make a little fire on the side of the tracks and cook food, whatever food we had or could find. We would stop in farmers' yards and grab a few potatoes and apples. One time the train started to move, and I had to struggle to get back on it. I could have escaped. But my sister was on the train, and I knew I had to get back on and take care of her.

Now, why else didn't I escape? I didn't escape because I was beaten down and had no place to go. First, I was extremely weak, tired, sick, and couldn't run. My knees would buckle. I had lice all over me. I was afraid to talk to anybody. I didn't trust any Germans. I couldn't go up to any Germans and ask, "Would you hide me?" They would probably turn me in or shoot me. At least this is what I believed. I didn't know what to do so I figured I'd stay on the train. Had I been alone, I might have done it. I was only 14 ½ years old at the time. I knew the train would soon be liberated. All I had to do was hold on.

One time the train stopped, and we had to all get out. American planes were going over strafing the train. We had to go and lay in the field, near the train. We didn't understand why they were shooting at the train. Apparently the Germans had hitched military machinery to the end of the train thus making it a military target, but I didn't understand this at the time.

Another time, we were at a town station, I don't remember which one, and all of a sudden bombs began hitting the railroad station. They told us to get out, and I jumped out of the train, took my sister, and we hid underneath the train. The bombs kept coming. After awhile, we were able to return to the train and a German officer gave us a lecture saying, "Wir siegen," which means we are still winning, don't you worry about it. The towns were in a shambles and wherever we went, for some reason or other, there were a lot of empty sardine cans. People were eating sardines. That's the only thing they had left. So, it was like walking through a place where there had been a major earthquake, old fighter planes would actually be laying around right in the middle of the town, and this guy is hollering at the top of his lungs about winning and that we would be in trouble then.

When we went through Berlin, we went very slowly but did not stop. We could see Berlin was like a ghost town. The Germans were still in control, but it was only a matter of a week or two before it would fall. When we looked out, all I could see of Berlin were these great big buildings. They were still standing, but they were all bombed out. Only the walls or some of the walls would be standing. One building after another, it was unbelievable. Other towns seemed all crumbled, but Berlin had all these shells of buildings and half buildings. I felt good about it. But my physical condition was so run down, that I couldn't feel much more than that. I had only two things on my mind: where to get food and how to get back to civilization. The first thing was to stay alive and the second thing was to get back. I could see that the Germans were losing but still trying to hang on. I just knew I had to stay alive until then and there would be hope. Each time we got to a town, we would hear that the town we had just been through before had been liberated by the Allies, mostly the British, but we didn't distinguish. Looking at the route of the train now, it headed mostly in an easterly direction but then turned south at Berlin. It could have been headed to Theresienstadt, but no one will really ever know.

Meantime, the train was getting emptier and emptier as bodies were removed every day. Everyone could have a seat at some point. One morning we were sleeping on the train, and a woman came running in saying, "We're free, we're free!" I couldn't believe my ears. I went outside and could see Russian soldiers taking away German guards.

70

Only a few guards were left. Most of them had fled in the night. The train began with 2500 prisoners and ended with 2000.

We asked the Russians what we should do. They told us to just go to the nearby town, Trobitz. The war was still going on and the Russians didn't have time to organize us. They weren't organization troops. They were front line troops, fighting infantry soldiers. So the two thousand of us who remained went to the town of Trobitz. The place was like a ghost town, no people, all empty houses. The German citizens had fled toward the advancing American troops because they were afraid of what the Russians might do who were close upon them from the East. We picked a house and moved into it.

We walked into this house and thought it was a nice house. I remember it must have been a barbershop because it had a barber chair in the corner. So, we just moved in and said, "We'll see what happens." Other people moved into the same house and here's one of the great coincidences of the war to me. The other person who moved into this house was the Lichtenfels' daughter, the same people that my mother and father and sister and I moved in with after losing our home in Lippstadt. What I don't understand is that I never saw her at the camp or on the train, but there she was. I almost fell over when I saw her. How could she get in that same house with us? I hadn't seen them since I left Germany in 1939, and this was 1945. So once again we were living in the same house.

But we had other problems to occupy us. We had no food. It seems like all I ever thought about was food. The war was still going on. We were now free, which was wonderful, but we had nothing to eat. So, I had to go find food. I would steal it from local farms. One time, I ran into an old lady at a farm and I told her I wanted some food. By this time, I was a little more bold. I didn't really beg. She gave me some bread and potatoes which I took back to the house.

71

Another time, I met some other kid from the camp around my age, and we decided to go looking for food together. We were walking along and ran into some Russian soldiers. They had half a pig that they had slaughtered. They asked us if we wanted part of it and we said okay. We were both very weak and couldn't walk very fast or carry much. But we decided to carry this pig. We were hauling it home to divide between him and me. I have never seen the other kid since until the 50th reunion trip in 1995 to trace The Lost Transport. There he was, sitting across the aisle from me on the bus. He now lives in Israel, and his son is a fighter pilot. We talked for a short time, exchanging memories.

Another time, three of us were looking for food and stole two bicycles owned by French officers. The three of us were on these two bikes. They came running after us and told us to stop, but we didn't. We started escaping with the bikes. They caught up to us and questioned us. I can't remember what questions they were asking. But, they hit one of the other kids so hard that the kid flew up against me and knocked me down. Then the French guy took the bike. That was that. I've never seen the other kids since either.

There were a lot of Russian soldiers coming through all the time on horseback, in tanks, on motorcycles, in trucks. We learned the Russian word for bread, which I have since forgotten, and whenever I saw them, I yelled, "Bread! Bread!" They would throw bread to me. Another time, I saw an old dog dish full of meat, and I don't even know if I was hungry or not. We were getting more food at that time. But whatever food I saw, I had to eat it. It might have been there two days or two weeks, but I ate it.

Soon the second wave of Russian troops came in, the organizing, occupying forces, and they said no more stealing food and no more this and that. They tried to establish some rules, some law. So, as I recall, we quit stealing. They gave us food.

People from the train pointed out Izzy's son who had snitched on the men from the neighboring compound who had tried to get on the train. The Russians arrested him and put him in jail.

I met a Russian soldier I could talk to. He said he was Jewish. He said that in Russia, they don't have any persecution of Jews. I thought that must be nice.

The Russians were deathly afraid of typhus, and we had these disease carrying lice all over us. The Russians decided to delouse us and they did a good job. They came to all of our houses and told us to get out and then sealed the place up and fumigated. They made us take all our clothes off and fumigated everything from this portable equipment they had. An hour later, I got my clothes back and the lice were gone. I couldn't believe it. The lice were totally gone. I had not one more louse. Neither did my sister. All the seams in the clothes were solid white, like stitches, nice ribbons. These were dead lice eggs. The Russians had killed all those too. They were like decorations, like strings, all along the seams. They were no longer harmful.

The delousing was in response to an outbreak of typhus that had begun. I remember the Lichtenfels girl got it and laid there for several days. Fevers were so high with typhus that the person would be delirious. Spots would also break out on the person's body, three spots on the stomach we were told. Then, I got it. I remember lying there half conscious, delirious with high fever. I can remember to this day lying there and not knowing what was going on. Ursula took care of me.

A Russian doctor visited me. I distinctly remember what he told me. He said, "You have to keep your heart going." He also told me that if I had remained captive under those conditions for another two or three weeks, I would have been dead. For medicine, he gave me a piece of chocolate as a stimulant, and I ate it. That's the only medicine I had. No aspirin or anything to get the fever down. Later when they weighed me, I was 76 pounds. I was 14 1/2 years old.

After several days of lying there, I got better, and I don't know if I'm imagining it, but I did see those three red

73

spots on my stomach. Ursula got it after me. I was better by this time and could help take care of her as she had helped to take care of me. She likely got it from me. But it was hard to avoid. So many of the people who had managed to survive the train trip went on to die of typhus.

We were located deep in the Russian zone. But then one day the Russians told everyone to get out into the street. We heard all this noise and then saw American trucks, quite a few, maybe as many as fifteen. These were deuce-and-a-halves. Two American soldiers were in each truck, one driving and one sitting on the fender. All of us were watching them come into Trobitz.

I remember that quite a few of the soldiers were black. When they stopped, I couldn't talk to them because I couldn't speak English. I said, "Hi," though, and they passed out some chocolate and they had big smiles. I was really impressed. Some of them had these great big brown belts on and they looked really sharp. Their helmets were kind of tilted to the side. I thought, "Well, that's why they won the war. These guys really know what to do." I didn't know all of the resources that this country has. I was just completely impressed with these American soldiers.

The Russians said that a bunch of people were going to the American zone. We should listen for our name to be called. When they called my name and Ursula's, we got on the truck. There were so many trucks, it seemed like a parade like on the Fourth of July. We were on our way to Leipzig. We had one sad incident on the way when one truck stopped suddenly causing a rear end collision where one of the American drivers was killed. Although Leipzig was in the American zone, according to the newest agreement, Leipzig would be under Russian occupation and the Americans would be farther west. When we arrived, signs were everywhere essentially saying, "Be nice to the Russians; The Russians will be here soon; Be nice to the Russians and they will treat us well."

Another one of the oddest coincidences in my life is how I even got on the trucks to Leipzig. Back in Eersel, one of my friends, Hans Raymakers' father was an officer in the Dutch Army attached to the American Army in Paris at the end of the war. The nuns in Eersel had no word of us and figured we were dead. My aunt and uncle in Chicago thought we must be dead also. After all, my aunt's whole family was dead, all of her brothers and sisters, everyone had disappeared. And so had we.

But Mr. Raymakers was sitting in Paris in his office going over lists of people from concentration camps from all over. Lo and behold, he came across George and Ursula Levy, survivors in Trobitz, among the Russians. The Russians had sent him the list. The first thing he did was wire the Russians to send us back to the west. He went on to send a telegram to my uncle in Chicago telling him it appeared we were alive and all right. And he sent a telegram to the nuns in Eersel as well as a telegram to Meneer v Mackelenbergh, our guardian. And that is how we ended up in Leipzig.

I must say I liked it there. We were staying at an ex-German Army camp that was for the purpose of maintaining a motor pool. They made us go through another delousing procedure despite the fact that the Russians had done a good job of it. We still had on our same clothes that we wore out of Bergen-Belsen. I had some old pants, a pair of socks, shoes, and a shirt or sweater, and a German Army overcoat. The Jewish star was still on some of them.

We stayed in a barracks and had total freedom to come and go as we pleased. I even took a street car into Leipzig once. The town was mostly rubble. I was also getting my strength back during this period. I could run some finally. But at night I would sweat something awful. My hair had turned gray at the age of fifteen, and I'm not completely sure about my appearance. Once in town, a woman made a scene about the appearance of my eyelashes saying, "Look at his eyelashes!" I didn't know what she was talking about.

Although I was propositioned by a Russian woman on the base, I was not interested in that still. I still was only interested in food. I always wanted more food. I waited for the American soldiers to come out of the mess tent. They emptied their plates into a drum and this was totally foreign to me, to take any kind of food and throw it away. I would eat out of there and then take the left-overs to my sister. One American soldier caught me doing this and ran after me. I thought, "Oh, well, I'm going to get shot or something." He asked me what I was doing and I told him. He told me to throw it away and took me into the mess tent and gave me a big dinner.

I became his friend and ate dinner with him everyday, sometimes two meals a day. He would not allow me to go to the garbage can. He gave me as much as I wanted and then I took some home to Ursula. I was very impressed with this white bread, Wonder Bread. I thought it was from heaven. He would give me white bread and chocolate, anything I wanted.

This soldier drove a truck and sometimes I rode around with him. He washed his sweater in gasoline. This is the truth. I was amazed at that, how they could wash a sweater in gasoline when I remember the Germans even back in 1943 were running buses on wood, gasoline was so precious. They carried a load on the buses that ran from Eersel to Eindoven. The driver would need to stop every twenty minutes to put wood in the stove in the back of his bus. And here was this guy washing his sweater in gasoline. And he would chew gum and spit it out, which I couldn't believe. He gave me gum also. I also used to walk behind the Americans and pick up any cigarette butts to roll these into cigarettes with a machine I had picked up. Then I sold them. The Americans had plenty of what were thought of as rare commodities in Leipzig.

Once this soldier took me to a dance where big band music was playing. I loved the music and spent the whole night hanging out there, watching people dance and listening.

I was also amazed about the radios on the Jeeps. I couldn't believe they had radios without any wires. All this stuff was new to me.

Staying in Leipzig was a pleasant time, and both my sister and I were getting stronger. We had enough to eat, and people were good to us. Essentially, I was free. I had to do what the Americans told me to, but I wasn't too worried about what was going to happen to me. I was just content to be, to have enough food, not to worry about dying, and not to worry about getting hit.

One day they put a big notice up and my name and my sister's were on it. Again, we were transported by truck and by train. But this was a happy occasion. We were going to Holland. Still in my concentration camp clothes with the dead lice eggs, I got on this train. Everybody was happy because we were going home.

Some people sat on top of the train, and I don't know if they did that because the train was so crowded or just because they wanted to sit there. But a couple people died when the train went under a viaduct. The train trip lasted about ten hours, I believe, and was the equivalent distance of going from Chicago to Omaha. We had enough to eat and everything was fine. Our destination in the Netherlands was the American base in Valkenburg. Everyone stood in line to be interviewed by a soldier behind a desk with no gun or anything. Just a guy in an office. I was amazed by that.

We, Ursula and I, were assigned to a barracks where we ate and slept. Every morning I would wake up in a pool of water with my sheets soaking wet from the sweat. When receiving a routine check by an American Army doctor, I told him about these sweats. He said, "That's from lack of protein. You're weak but as your body gets better, this will stop." And it did.

We stayed at the base in Valkenburg perhaps a week. Finally, I wanted to get back to Eersel. The sad part about it was I didn't have a home to go to. Meneer v. Mackelenbergh lived quite a ways from there, maybe fifty miles. My real home in Germany was gone along with both my parents. I didn't quite know where to go, but I knew I had to go some place. I couldn't stay in Valkenburg with the Americans forever. I told the Americans I wanted to go to Den Bos to see my guardian, v. Mackelenbergh. I was given some money and a train ticket and headed to Den Bos with Ursula.

Sunday morning we arrived at the train station in Den Bos, and we walked from the train station to the v. Mackelenbergh house where they lived upstairs. We rang the bell. They opened the door and said, "Who is it?" I said, "It's George and Ursula," and all pandemonium broke out. They had no idea where we were although they had heard we were alive and in the Russian sector. They were so glad to see us even though we looked horrible. Me with my gray hair and our clothes still the concentration camp clothes with the dead lice eggs, we looked a sight. I had been out of the camp for probably a total of eight to ten weeks. The first six weeks or so was spent in Trobitz. This would make it approximately the end of June, beginning of July, 1945. The v. Mackelenberghs took a look at our clothes and practically ripped them off our backs. Off went my German Army coat and the dirty pants and the same underwear that I had probably worn for two years, and they put it all in a pile. Then they burned those clothes, right there on the roof garden of their house. I saw the flames.

Following this, they put me and my sister in two separate hospitals. Ursula went to the same hospital where my Uncle Joseph had worked back in 1938 – 1939 before leaving for the United States. And everyone there remembered him and spoke well of him. All I did in the hospital was lay there and eat – they wanted to fatten me up. The v. Mackelenberghs visited me on a regular basis. I would get up and walk around and had regular visits from doctors.

I remember that they put me in a bathtub. I know I had two years of dirt on me even though we had those showers at Bergen-Belsen. They weren't good showers. This Catholic brother put me in the bathtub and took a big scrub brush, the kind you scrub floors with, and he just brushed me with soap and water like brushing the floor. Afterwards, back to bed I went.

After gaining some weight, they sent me back to Eersel to live at St. Jacobus. Ursula was in the girls' section which was very restricted. However, in the boys' section, I had a lot of freedom. I was able to go to town and visit my friends, stay at their houses, things like that. I took up with my old friends, Sjef Blox, Ties Quinten, Hans Raymakers, and the Van Dyke family. We generally met at the Van Dyke bakery. So, during the day, I was able to go into town and live like a normal human being.

But my parents were the nuns, so to speak. Father Leo Weyers was still there and continued to befriend us as before we were taken away. Throughout the summer of 1945 this was my life. In the fall, Ursula went to school in Eersel and I went away again to the school, fifth grade, at The Ruwenberg. I had gained weight, and my hair was turning from gray to black.

All the other German kids that originally had fled and lived at St. Jacobus were gone by now. Some of them, however, I am in contact with to this date. But most of them were half Jewish and returned to Germany. Except there was Ilse Brul and Inge Brul. Out of everyone staying at St. Jacobus, Ilse Brul was the only one lost in the camps, dead.

My sister and I, having been there for so long, more than all the other refugee kids from Germany, were considered a part of the town. We were thought of as one with the town. I spoke Dutch totally without an accent like I was born there, and so did Ursula.

One thing that had changed at St. Jacobus since we had left was that Mother Renildus had been reassigned. The new Mother at St. Jacobus was into the details and rules of religion in a way that Mother Renildus was not. This new woman would never have been a flamboyant Dutch resistance fighter. Mother Renildus, who had done so much during the war, had moved on. She was, I'm convinced, the right woman at the right time in history.

After our return to Eersel, my Uncle Joseph and Aunt Irmgard kept in close touch with us. My uncle wrote us often from the United States. He even managed a long distance diagnosis that proved correct. The nuns told him that my sugar was high in blood tests, but Uncle Joseph said don't worry about it, he's not diabetic. This is just the result of the sudden nutrition I was getting by now. He turned out to be correct. Uncle Joseph was an excellent doctor.

He also sent us packages with food and novel items. For instance, he sent peanut butter which was like having something rare such as gold or diamonds. Everyone was fascinated with these jars of peanut butter he sent. I gave everyone a taste. And he sent me pants with a zipper. Everyone wanted to see my zipper and I had to unzip my zipper all the time to show everyone how it worked. Everyone else had buttons back then. And another small thing – he sent Ivory soap. It floats. Everyone wanted to see it float. These things, apparently common in America, none of us had seen before.

When we returned to Eersel, we also found out yet another story on what had happened to our mother, Lucie Hope Levy. A cousin now in the United States reported that my mother did not die when we thought, before we even left Eersel, but survived until almost the end of the war. My cousin Margaret was in the concentration camps of Riga and then later Stuthoff with my mother. She said my mother, even under the circumstances, was always a happy person, had a kind word for everyone, and was very full of hope. Eventually, Margaret and my mother were both sent elsewhere, to separate camps. My mother, I thought, had been sent to the camp in Riga, Latvia, where about one month before liberation, she was seen on a pile of dead. In reality, she died in Stuthoff, as indicated on her gravestone, around two months or so later than we thought.

I couldn't believe it that she had been alive until practically the Russians had arrived. If she had lived another month or so, she would have survived.

In early 1947, Meneer v. Mackelenbergh had me come to his house in Den Bos and said, "I have something to tell you." He told me I was going to the United States and, this is hard to believe now, I did not want to go. He said I had to go. "You and your sister have to go. Your uncle wants you over there." Even though I was living at St. Jacobus, Eersel had truly been a home to me. Life seemed very nearly normal now. I had friends. I have no doubt, even today, that I could have made some kind of happy life in Eersel. So, I was told, whether you like it or not, you are going to the United States. There were no if, ands, or buts about it.

We got ready to go.

Leaving Holland, 2000

True to the story of his life, George's leaving of Holland to come to the United States was rather dramatic. And not surprisingly, over fifty years later when our little group went to leave Holland and return to the United States, we also had our small drama, the only hitch in Katie's meticulously planned trip.

Our hotel reservation had somehow been lost by the hotel. We were planning to stay near Amsterdam in order to catch our planes the next afternoon to Chicago or Detroit. We stood in a long line at Schiphol Airport seeing what kind of accommodations were available and the quick version is – none. Even youth hostels had filled. Amsterdam was one busy town from the center to at least fifty miles out. Having survived typical travelers' hazards like occasional mediocre food, a flat tire on the rental van, death defying feats on the autobahn, and cold North Sea winds, we had no place to stay on our last night in Europe. We stood there with the inevitable accumulation of extra baggage from forays in overpriced gift shops, thinking of temporarily abandoned children, husbands, and rat terriers, and discussed our options. George settled the matter. "We'll just spend the

81

night here at the airport. After all, it's not Bergen-Belsen." Indeed, it's not. We all agreed. But sitting up all night at Schiphol is an experience of its own.

Day turns to night and night heads toward that dead zone that echoes with emptiness – regular folk including flight crews having found other refuge. The denizens of the night include a smattering of stuporized fellow travelers, the night shift at the all night coffee stand clinking newly washed dishes, floor sweepers, nearly invisible security personnel, and one imagines a mouse or two creeping along the edges willing to risk exposure for those extra biscotti crumbs globe trotting yuppies have left in their wake.

A good sized cockroach is emboldened by the hour and moves with impressive speed from under the bench where Sue sleeps and skitters across the tiled floor. I resist the urge to point it out, but Sue opens her eyes in time to catch its get-away and raises her eyebrows in my direction. Birds chirp softly in the rafters, the only creatures flying now. The occasional night-crew conversation in Dutch wafts through the air and another night traveler holds her coffee close, willing the caffeine from the cup through the air directly into her lungs.

My companions, on the whole, have conked out on the hot pink and mauve upholstered benches intended for coffee customers. Dan reads, and I've just finished sorting coins into two piles: one for coins marked Deutschland and the other for coins marked Nederlands. I'll swap them for dollars in the morning.

George, meantime, sleeps undisturbed on the bench across the way. Katie is restless but dozes off from time to time. Amy snoozes. I drink numerous cups of cappuccino and stay up all night. But George clearly gets the prize for sound sleeping.

Earlier today (or was it yesterday?) we attended commemorative proceedings at Camp Westerbork, the transit camp. Elderly rabbis, young and old family members, camp survivors both tearful and stoic, made their way along what for some was old familiar ground, past the appel platz where they once stood for roll call, and on to the end of the railway track where human cargo was dispersed to the concentration camps. Some came to remember; some perhaps to finally put memories to rest. They came to say Kaddish for those long lost.

We finished off the last supplies of mints, granola bars, hard candies, and apple slices before finally ending up here at what we were jokingly calling the Hotel Schiphol, fellow pilgrims making our way back home. We decided that the rooms are large, the price is right, we have unlimited hot water in the bathrooms, and the seats are of first class size. Pancakes and duty free shops will entice us in the morning, and we will arise to the aroma of freshly brewed coffee.

George, with great tenderness, turns to Katie in the middle of the night and tells her, "I love you," as though they were in some romantic hide-away. We all head home on time the next day, George determined to make a lunch date with his distant cousin Margaret and finally get to the bottom of his mother's story, the full truth of which was yet to be discovered.

Part Five – Integration: Old Life and New

But, above all, man is a personality, a spirit incarnate, an open relation to the totality of all that is. As such, he far transcends the world of his environment. And his final integration transcends his everyday integration.

(Bernard J. Boelen, *Personal Maturity:*
The Existential Dimension)

Leaving Eersel, 1947

The nuns took pictures and threw us a big farewell party as we were ready to leave for America. A picture of myself and Ursula leaving for America hangs on the wall in their picture gallery today along with a picture of Ilse Brul and Mother Renildus.

We flew to America from Eindhoven and Amsterdam. My uncle arranged and paid for everything. The pilot let me sit in the cockpit with him for a time, and I was really impressed with that. He also radioed ahead to New York that there were two DP ("displaced persons") children traveling alone coming in on the plane which was a novelty at the time. March 19, 1947, we landed in New York and stepped off the plane to flashing light bulbs and interviews. I was sixteen and Ursula was eleven. Apparently, they considered us kids having been through the war like that and arriving in America big news. Reporters asked questions like, "What is it you want right now?" and I said, "Well, I'd take some of that Chiklets gum." He bought me around ten boxes of Chiklets gum, and I was in heaven. And I also said I would like a car. The next day, the news was in all the New York papers with headlines like, "George says, he would like a car." I was assured that didn't mean

I'd get one. My uncle had arranged for someone to meet us at the airport to put us up until it was time for our plane to Chicago.

We landed in Chicago at Midway Airport on a dark and rainy night. Uncle Joseph and Aunt Irmgard met us along with more press. Articles appeared in all the Chicago papers.

The next day, Uncle Joseph took me with him when he went to make rounds at Grant Hospital. He had me wait in the coffee shop while he saw patients. All these newspapers were there and our picture was on the back page. I was sitting there minding my own business, not understanding anything, waiting for my uncle, and a lady began pointing at the newspaper and at me. Everyone in the coffee shop came over and started talking to me and looking at me, asking me questions that I couldn't understand. I was so embarrassed, I didn't know what to do. Uncle Joseph came back about then and rescued me, talking to the people. We got in the car and I said, "I don't know if I want this. I don't like this."

My aunt insisted that I should be productive, and I went through a series of jobs over the next couple of years such as elevator operator, bus boy, dishwasher, dry cleaner delivery boy, and I didn't keep any of them long. I didn't know English and was physically still weak.

But my uncle said you have to do something in this world, and he sent me to a tutor to learn English. My uncle aggressively moved me from one school to another virtually demanding of the high school that I graduate on time. So I did in 1949. I also managed to play tuba in a band, play baseball, and get myself elected vice-president of the class despite knowing very little English. I think everyone felt sorry for me.

My uncle gave me a choice of colleges to attend, and I picked St. Mary's in Winona, Minnesota. All the freshmen rode a special train, the Hiawatha, from Chicago to St. Mary's. I went to St. Mary's for four years which was a turning point for me. I finally felt something good was happening to me. I made friends there that I still keep, and I met Katie there.

It was important for me to feel normal and clearly my past was not normal. All I needed was the memory of all those reporters to let me know that. I kept my past strictly to myself not telling anyone the whole truth.

After graduating from St. Mary's with a degree in Economics in 1953, I was drafted into the United States Army and served from 1953 – 1955. I was stationed near Paris for a while and had a chance to visit old friends in Holland and even took the train from Paris to Lippstadt one time staying at the Drei Kronen. My father's old friends or "friends," I was never sure which, recognized me when I stopped for a drink at the old bowling alley tavern. They came around me all excited telling me how much they loved my father, Max. I was profoundly uncomfortable with this and left.

Until I went to the 50th reunion at Bergen-Belsen and the camps, I never felt anyone truly could understand what Ursula and I had been through. But, there I met people who really understood, who knew exactly, not just somewhat, but exactly what we went through. In many ways, that experience has allowed me to lay it to rest.

I talk to children in schools, have visited several of my grandchildren's classes to tell them about the Holocaust. But I'm no philosopher. I don't philosophize *nothing*. I just tell what happened. I think it's enough.

Lucie's Fate Discovered, 2000

Upon our return from Holland, George decided to meet with his cousin, Margaret Oppenheimer, who also lives in the Chicago area. He was ready to hear the sequence of events that really happened to his mother. Up to this point, he had had two different stories and, after locating the memorial stone in the Lippstadt cemetery, he figured he still didn't know the truth. Margaret is the person with the most reliable information on this.

Margaret softly told her story and the story of Lucie Hope Levy. All Jews in the Lippstadt area were reduced to living in two specified houses, called Juden Hauses, and Margaret's mother's house in Olde was one of those. After putting Ursula and George on the Kindertransport, Lucie lived there along with another woman and two extra families. This was 1939. Margaret was fifteen.

In November of 1939, Margaret left for a Jewish orphanage where she was trained as a nurse and didn't see everyone again until 1941. She had made her way home by this time. The mayor of the town ordered a resettlement of all the Jews in town. He wanted them out, in other words. They were taken from their homes on December 10, 1943, and pushed into trains on December 13, 1943. Margaret had the job of handing out bread during the train ride. But on this train, she didn't see her mother or Lucie until arriving in Riga.

An area of the town of Riga, Latvia, had been isolated as a Jewish ghetto with restricted freedom of movement. This is where Margaret, her mother, Lucie, and others went. When they arrived, they were directed to houses that were empty but food was still on the tables. It turned out that the Nazis killed 26,000 Latvian Jews to make room for the new incoming German Jews.

During this time at Riga, she as well as Lucie worked during the day although she doesn't recall what kind of factory job Lucie had. This was forced labor, of course. They would try to get a hold of things that could be bartered for food.

Everyone was concerned for Margaret's mother because she was growing weaker but would not, for example, eat horse meat no matter what. One day, Margaret bartered for a wonderful piece of horse meat which she brought home. Lucie somehow came up with the ingredients to make sauerbraten out of the meat, and Margaret's mother ate it with gusto. Afterwards, Margaret couldn't resist telling her mother what she had eaten. Her mother immediately went outside and threw the food up declaring that she would never trust them again about food. She was angry with Margaret. This argument was never resolved. To this day, Margaret wishes that she had heard her mother say, "I forgive you," for that trick, but her mother died shortly afterwards.

Margaret told how Lucie's personality remained exactly as George remembered it – cheerful, fun-loving, and kind to everyone even in these difficult circumstances. No matter how bad everyone was feeling, Lucie would successfully cheer them up. She sang all the time and especially loved singing, "We'll hang our wash out on the Siegfried Line."

Both women, Margaret and Lucie, eventually ended up in the concentration camp of Stuthoff described by Margaret as "a bad one." Margaret talked to Lucie once over a fence in August of 1944. Lucie died in Stuthoff, not Riga, and there are no eyewitnesses, apparently, putting her on a pile of dead at either location near the end of the war. According to Margaret, it is possible that Lucie lived that long as her health looked good in August 1944. But this cannot be confirmed.

So, George has found some answers but can never, in all probability, resolve exactly when his mother died. At least he knows she kept her spirits up close to the end of the war, and he knows now where she died. But one piece of comfort is that George really believes he takes after his mother in his ability to cheer people up and make a bad situation tolerable. In this respect, and in respect to his and Katie's five children and fifteen grandchildren, Lucie Hope Levy and her husband Max live on.

* * * * * *

On a trip to Glen Ellyn to go over revisions with George, we took time out to visit his son Joe and his wife Maureen. Their daughter Phoebe was having a little family birthday gathering. Everyone stood in the dimly lit dining room while Phoebe blew out the candles on her cake. George rested against a wall, jaunty, confident, a man at peace, a contented man, watching his granddaughter and family. Everything about the moment was life affirming, and George was the patriarch of this group of birthday celebrants. The three generations in the room were tightly bound to the future.

Afterword: Family Voices

Sundays too my father got up early [and]
Made banked fires blaze.
What did I know, what did I know
Of love's austere and lonely offices?

(Robert Hayden,
"Those Winter Sundays")

George and Katie raised five children:
- Jane, a pharmacist, married to Tom, an orthodontist;
- Sue, a pharmacist married to Tim a pharmacist;
- Joe, a doctor, married to Maureen, the lone humanities person in this family;
- Lucy, a nurse-midwife, married to Craig, a partner in a consulting firm;
- Amy, a nurse, married to Dan, a partner in an orthotics firm.

If you imagine a pattern here, you're right. Not only has each child focused his or her career in some area related to science and medicine, but each has also married once and only once. Each of the couples has three children for a total of fifteen grandchildren for George and Katie. All five children stay in touch with each other and their parents via e-mail pretty much every day and seem to be a close family who each value re-creating a close family.

After all the children were grown and after he had three grandchildren, George found himself in a dangerous depression. Up until then, his Holocaust experiences were kept very private. Working through his issues with Dr. Boelen, George's old philosophy professor, old memories

90

surfaced. The children's contributions make references to this time. When asked to write something for this book that speaks to their experiences as the child of a survivor, each responded. Each emphasized that an important change had occurred with George as a result of the 50th Anniversary trip. Katie frames the picture of that all-important trip, and each child shares his or her thoughts.

Katie's Memories of the 50th Anniversary Trip

George received a letter from an old friend, Klaus Reichenbach, a Catholic priest living near Cologne. The letter told about a 50th reunion trip for Dutch Jews who survived the train trip which left Bergen-Belsen during the last weeks of the war. This train wandered over Germany as George has already recounted.

At first George agreed to go on this reunion trip and our son, Joe, said, "I'm going, too." Our daughters Lucy and Jane quickly joined up, and Maureen, Joe's wife, wasn't about to sit home if Joe was going to Europe, so she said, "Me, too."

Tickets were purchased, reservations made, baby sitters arranged. Our two daughters, Amy and Sue, felt terrible because they were unable to come at this time, but we assured them we would go another time with them which, as you've read, we did in 2000.

The night before we were all to leave, with our suitcases packed, dogs kenneled, and intricate plans made about meeting places as we prepared to gather in Europe from three different states, George stated emphatically, "I'm not going. Absolutely not." He said it would be too depressing, like a funeral. I did some fast talking and said, "It won't be depressing like a funeral but more like an Irish wake. You'll see people you remember and haven't seen for fifty years, and they will remember you, too. And besides there's no backing out. You have to go. You have no choice."

So, with some grumbling, off we went to the event that changed his life in a most remarkable way. It turned out George found the ultimate support group in the group pilgrimage from Holland to Westerbork to Bergen-Belsen and on to Trobitz.

We began the trip in April 1995. Joe, Mo, George, and I took off from O'Hare and headed to Amsterdam to meet Lucy who was on her way from Atlanta. We were all a little nervous. None of the kids had been to Europe yet and their thoughts were of their children left at home. Jane was leaving from Madison a day later to meet us in Lippstadt. George was nervous about the whole thing, and I was tired having worked for months on all the details of the trip.

We would not travel from Amsterdam with the official tour – four bus loads of survivors, their children, and family members. Instead, we picked Lucy up at customs in Schiphol and headed for a full day of tourist activities in Amsterdam. I figured a little tourism and fun would keep us on the level during more intense times.

After a canal boat ride, we went to Anne Frank's house. To be in the same rooms where she had lived was incredible. It was very quiet. People whispered and used low voices. We looked out the attic window where she stood looking at the outside world. We found it emotional and moving.

We finished a full day of tourism following the next morning by more with our trip to Keukenhof. Then, we started off for Lippstadt but decided instead to head northeast to Westerbork. The bus tour would be there the next day, so we had the place pretty much to ourselves. George was our guide showing us where his barracks had been, where he stood at appel twice a day, and where the tracks ended and unloaded the prisoners. We visited the museum to see photos of the actual camp with its buildings and triple high wooden bunks. We all had tears in our eyes when he translated the memorial at the end of the tracks: *They gave us every burden so that we could not fulfill our destiny.*

Our days were over.   ***Yes, our end had come.***
(Lamentations 4:18.)

During the several hours we spent at Westerbork, George was treated with great respect by the museum curators who questioned him about his time spent there. We left late in the afternoon and made the four hour trip to Lippstadt where we met Jane at the Drei Kronen.

The next morning after a good German breakfast of hard rolls, salami, cheese, soft boiled eggs, and plenty of strong coffee, we ventured around town. Eventually, we stopped at the town bakery and there was Friedel Meyer, George's childhood friend. After much hand shaking, hugging, and posing for pictures, fresh baked cookies and pastries were passed around. We were also able to meet with Hans Boenicke this trip too.

Eventually, we left Lippstadt and headed to Braunschweig to join the Lost Transport group and attend the official welcome of the German government. The mayor and other government officials gave speeches. As we walked toward the hall, George was visibly nervous, but as he looked toward a group headed toward us, he called out, "Mr. Melkman!" There he was, the very man who had befriended him fifty years ago. He looked great even though he was in his eighties, the oldest survivor on the trip. They hugged and grinned and hugged some more. They couldn't stop looking and smiling at, touching each other.

The next morning, we joined the English speaking group on Bus # 3 and headed toward Bergen-Belsen some thirty miles away. The bus was, at first, quiet, but as people began speaking to each other, things loosened up. We met a family from Boston and people began to exchange information. Some on the bus were actual survivors who had been in the camps but most were family members who had come to represent their dead relatives who had originally survived the camps.

As we approached Bergen-Belsen in our luxury buses, it became quiet and some spoke of their thoughts and feelings about the last time fifty years ago that they had come that way. We walked slowly and quietly on the path to the memorial obelisk erected on the first anniversary of the liberation. We passed many large mass burial mounds. There were prayers, chants, and speakers, and many tears from all. Later, the workers in the museum were gracious, courteous, and helpful and gave freely of their books about the camp and photocopies of lists of names to all survivors or family members.

Later that evening in Braunschweig, George got acquainted with more survivors exchanging stories and memories. I was right – it was much like an Irish wake, meeting old friends with much talking about the "old days."

The next day we drove to Potsdam for more official dinners and speeches. One event was held in the very room where Truman, Churchill, and Stalin had their famous conference after the war. The kids skipped some of these solemn occasions and caught a train into Berlin to have a brew, watch the people, and experience the city.

The next morning, we split up. George, Lucy, and I rode the bus. Joe, Mo, and Jane followed in the van. We all headed to Trobitz. We took back roads and sped along behind our police escort. Sirens were blaring, the sound giving the survivors the creeps as fifty year old memories of police sirens came back. On the several hour drive, we also had a helicopter escort as some threats had been made concerning the safety of the buses.

During the long drive, people on the buses were encouraged to stand up and share their personal stories with the group which had the effect of drawing them all together as a unit. When George told his story about he and another boy carrying the pig, the man across the aisle called out, "I was the one who helped you." Some stories were funny, but most brought tears to our eyes.

When we arrived in Trobitz, the townspeople opened up to all of us. Teens served as guides. George found the house where he and Ursula had lived. After a memorial was dedicated, there was more exploring done. We found the train tracks which had brought them to the town. We took many pictures and lots of addresses and phone numbers were exchanged. Hugs and handshakes were given.

The four buses pulled out and we, emotionally drained, returned to our van to make our way as tourists again back to Amsterdam and the good old U.S. of A. Our spirits lifted as we went on, and George repeated over and over that a weight was lifted from his back.

Sue

I remember my dad always starting to talk about the Holocaust and then saying, "I'll tell you when you're older." It became a common phrase – almost a joke. How old did I have to be?

I always felt my dad and, therefore, maybe myself were different from others, different in a good way, a special way, a private way. I was proud of him and felt protective about his past and still am. It's like people have to earn the right to know about him. It's a privilege for people to find out, and I have to really trust and respect somebody before I talk about it. I'm getting better about trembling when I talk about it, but I usually do and sometimes my mouth trembles so much it's hard to speak. My dad is a hero, my hero. You couldn't have a more perfect role model in your life.

When my dad became depressed, I always thought it was for many reasons, but not mainly from his past. That's so weird to think about now. I thought it was from his eyesight getting worse, becoming a grampa three times, his job situation, and also from his past. But it wasn't the main reason, I thought. That's because I really didn't know much about his past to have a true grasp at how horrible it was. Even though I saw those movies in German class that showed the huge piles of dead bodies, and I always thought, "My dad was there," it wasn't real to me. Now it is.

I will always regret not going on the trip for the 50th anniversary reunion. Or maybe it's guilt that I feel. But everyone who went on it has a special bond, and I know it "cleansed" my dad in a way. I'm so glad that I did go on this last trip. I'll always have that and can't wait to take my family there to show them all of this history.

I see myself as different from others because of my dad. I view it as a positive difference, a benefit, kind of like I'm on the sideline with most people. I'm proud "to be Jewish" and I think I'm more sensitive to prejudice than most people. It really bothers me deep down, more intensely than most I think. I almost have a fetish about people who think that they are better than others. I just can't tolerate that and won't consider a person like that as a friend. I am highly sensitive to anti-Semitism and also have an inner feeling of pity for people who say those things to me.

My kids are very interested in the subject of the Holocaust and their grandfather. At first I was oh so eager to tell all, and I did. There is so much to teach them in all of this. But I also became leery and protective when their friends started saying certain things and after knowing the hatred is still out there. It's a fine line. You never know what could happen. I know that they have the same sense of honor that I have for my dad. I can tell.

I think I have an ideal family. I'm so proud of my sisters and brother that I find it hard not to brag about them. I want so much for my kids to have the same childhood that I had. I also feel a tremendous love and honor for my mom and dad. I'm proud of them. I'm glad that I inherited some of their traits. I take pride that I inherited certain qualities of my dad's such as his sense of humor, common sense, optimism, and his young at heart outlook on life. He can always make me laugh. He is a wonderful dad. I try to live up to him, and when I see him in myself, I'm happy.

Lucy

As a small child, what I remember most is related to food. I always remember my dad saying, "You don't know what it is to be hungry" when we wouldn't finish our meals.

Although I didn't fully understand it at the time, I knew that what he was saying had something very serious behind it. He couldn't stand wasting anything and had a real hard time if he thought we didn't appreciate how nice our lives were.

I always knew that he was Jewish as a child and was in the camps, but it was never discussed in any detail. As I grew older, maybe high school, he would tell an occasional story and I was just beginning to understand. I remember watching a Holocaust movie with him in our basement. He sat silently throughout the entire movie, very out of character. At the end, he stood up and said, "Those ----ing bastards," and went upstairs. It was the first time I had ever seen him express such hate toward the Nazis but he never said anything else about it.

When I saw the movie, "Sophie's Choice," I came home and told him about it. I thought it was so unthinkable and awful, and he reacted with a casual statement like, "That was nothing. Stuff like that happened all the time."

Growing up, I always felt a connection to the Jewish part of my heritage. I felt special for being named Lucy after his mother. Many times he said I was just like her – fun-loving, making people laugh – which made me feel good. Sometimes he also told me I was like his sister, Ursula, which left me with mixed feelings. He seemed proud of her in many ways, but also seemed to have unresolved issues left over from their experiences together during the war.

I always felt my dad had something out of the ordinary about him but couldn't really identify it. I admired the fact that he always seemed cooler than the other dads and all my friends thought he was great. But I resented his mood swings and what seemed to be his irrational disciplinary measures.

When I went to college I started taking courses in Judaism and Jewish history and remember feeling like all the puzzle pieces were beginning to come together. I thought I was beginning to understand a lot of his behavior that as a young adolescent seemed unusual. I felt he never really had a childhood or role model as a young teenager and this

97

seemed to explain why he reacted what seemed to be strangely to situations that I thought didn't warrant such a reaction. "Forgiveness" isn't the right word but understanding and acceptance probably are. I felt I understood and accepted him more. I had a sense of calm and relief.

When my dad became depressed I immediately thought it was related to the Holocaust. Just prior to his depression, his store was burglarized although nothing was stolen. Everything was damaged. I remember telling my mom and dad about the connection and how he must have felt those same feelings of persecution and how this probably triggered his depression. They both thought it was a silly idea at the time and didn't think the two events were related. To tell you the truth, I don't know how they feel about it now. We didn't talk about it after that. I was living in Philadelphia and felt helpless not being able to help either my mom or dad. I wondered if I should fly home but it didn't seem like the right thing to do. I would talk to them on the phone. I remember once my dad telling me that Joe, my brother, was the only one helping him and that made me feel pretty rotten.

As to the reunion trip, I knew immediately I was going to go along. I didn't realize before the trip what it was really about and what affect it would have on my life and my relationship with my dad. Although he was reluctant, I knew he would go.

The part of the trip that affected me most were the bus rides between places and events. We were on the English speaking bus. During these rides, anyone who wanted to speak would stand in the front of the bus with a microphone and speak their mind. The stories and questions I heard on the bus rides made it all so real for me in a very personal way. The town and camp speeches and ceremonies were also moving, especially Bergen-Belsen, but it was on these bus rides that I really started to understand what I was experiencing and how real and important it all was. This was such a moving experience. I even stood in the front of the bus during one drive because I wanted everyone to know how much I appreciated their acceptance. We were the only Catholic people on the trip, but everyone accepted us as family and made us feel welcome and loved.

There was also often a sense of humor during the trip which I hadn't expected. It might seem morbid to talk about it as part of this emotional trip, but I think it was a release for all of us and enabled us to gather strength to deal with the horror of why we were there. My brother's joke cracked us all up. He said, "I hope they have a gift shop in Bergen-Belsen so I can get a tee shirt that says, 'My father went to Bergen-Belsen and all he got me was this lousy tee shirt.'"

I think the trip made my dad realize it was okay, even necessary, to talk about his experiences. I remember him saying how surprised he was at how normal everyone's life was, the other survivors, and how maybe he's okay after all.

I definitely don't shy away from my heritage. I tell about my dad's experiences often. I think it's important for people to know and it's the least I can do if that makes sense. Once at a 4th of July party, I met the father of a neighbor who had a German accent, and we started talking about Europe. I told him my dad was born in Germany but had lived in Holland for a few years. He told me he loved Holland and that he was part of Hitler's Army when they invaded Holland. I was so shocked, I asked him to repeat it and then just walked away. That was one of the only times I remember not saying anything about my heritage when maybe I should have.

I think my dad is a great and special man. I think he denied the atrocities of his childhood long enough to give us a normal and happy childhood. When I was little I used to think he was pretty cool and quite kid like. Since he's been on this trip and started talking about his experiences, I think he's become the man he was trying to be for all those years I was growing up. He's content, accepting, honest, trusting, non-judgmental, and giving. He often talks about all the great qualities of his Uncle Joseph Mueller but doesn't realize that he has most of those same qualities. I wish I were more like him in a lot of ways. Of course, that gives me some goals to work toward.

Amy

I remember always knowing that my dad was a Holocaust survivor even though I didn't really know what that meant. I thought it meant that Jewish people were killed for not believing in God the way Hitler did and so he put them into prisons and later killed them. I didn't have much to go on as far as knowing what really happened to him. His stories were brief and usually ended with, "I'll tell you more when you get older."

A few stories were often told such as the man trying to sneak into a line before a transport out of Bergen-Belsen and being shoved under barbed wire until he looked like hamburger meat. Or the story of how his mother put him on the train and told him to take care of Ursula and that she would see him soon. The stories never had an explanation before or after, but rather seemed like horrible memories randomly told.

As a child I didn't know anything about the Holocaust except what my dad had told me. I understood that I wasn't supposed to talk about his past to anyone, which was hard for me. I wanted to know more but when I would ask questions I would get one of the stories and not much else. I felt like I had this unbelievable secret, and I was afraid to talk about it, because if I told anyone, they might think something bad about my dad or family or just be shocked, and that isn't what I was after. I just wanted to understand more.

When my dad was depressed, I was a college student, all self absorbed. I felt that I had something to do with it by all the arguing I did with him. I'm sure it didn't help. For many years family and school distracted my dad and he was able to handle things as they came along. Now that his kids were all basically out of the house and his wife was working, it was too hard for him to put his past away to deal with current life. And I do believe that certain situations tipped him into depression though it seemed so obvious to me that his past was the real cause. I felt totally helpless during this time. I was home for the summer and remember one morning getting ready for work and trying to get him off the couch to go to work. I was telling him he had to go, and he just stood there crying and apologizing to me. I had nothing to say. I just sat there thinking this is my dad and he is crying and I don't know what to do. I was scared but didn't talk about it. I didn't think I should.

When the anniversary trip came up, my family was in the middle of deciding whether to move to Georgia or not. At the time, the trip didn't seem to be as big a deal as it turned out to be. I was reluctant to leave my family for that long and looking back now, I could kick myself. When they all came back from the trip they all seemed different in a good way. When they left, it seemed like a puzzle was dumped out and all the pieces were mixed up. But when they returned, the puzzle was being put together and they were all part of it. Things seemed organized for my dad. Talking to and seeing people who were actually from his past gave him something nobody else had been able to give him for fifty years. Imagine trying to explain something for fifty years and nobody having a clue what you are saying. He found that on the trip and I'm so glad he did. It was now okay to talk about his past and so began this book.

Growing up I never missed church as far as I can remember. My dad sometimes went with us but he slept through the sermon and always had a pocket of candy to eat during mass. On one side of me was my mom, serious about mass, and the other side was my dad who didn't seem to care if he was there or not. I never even thought it was strange if he didn't go and I knew it was my mom who felt strongly about following the rules of the Catholic Church. I don't feel as Catholic as I did growing up, but I think more about being a good person and less about following the rules of the Catholic church. As an adult I see myself having choices. I

101

understand now that there are no right or wrong answers in religion. I came to this understanding as a result of realizing that my dad isn't a Jew or a Catholic, but a man. And what he believes or doesn't believe shouldn't define him. This same realization has made me sensitive to anti-Semitic remarks. I feel like the people around me who say such things are just stupid but in the same thought, it scares me that people still feel that way enough to say it.

My family seems pretty normal. We all get along and talk frequently. Family has always been very important to my parents. I remember my dad always saying he wanted a big family. I would describe my dad as many things. First he is a dad. He has always been supportive and someone I knew I could go to with anything good or bad to work out. He is talented, playing many instruments, some at the same time. He is the only person I know who enjoys the finer things in life not because it is the thing to do, but because he truly enjoys them, and mostly my dad is content. He never complains or has regrets. I try and remember that every day when I let life's little problems get me down. Everyday I think about what he went through and it puts things in perspective that life is good, and I should appreciate all that I have.

Jane

When I was a child, my dad did not discuss the Holocaust much. He would occasionally use it to make a point or to put things in perspective for us. If he saw us wasting food or being overly picky at dinner, he would remind us that he ate sawdust and wood while at the camp. It definitely made an impression on me and would put a damper on things in my mind.

He did often tell us about his years in Eersel and the happy times he had with his boyhood friends there. He told us about Christmas traditions in Holland and sang songs to us in Dutch. When I was in the sixth grade, he came to my

classroom and gave a speech about Hollar
front blackboard and sang a child's song
little dance with it. I was simultanec
amazed at how unique he was compa
fathers. I'm certain he was the most po¡
that year. The teacher and the students abs.

They didn'
this con
boggl

I have always thought my dad was ,
proud of his background and heritage. It did se।
apart from the average suburban family. One unfortunate
thing, in my opinion, is that although my dad is fluent in
both German and Dutch, none of us kids learned a word of
either growing up. I understand perfectly well why he never
spoke to us in German, but I do wish he could have taught us
a little Dutch. I guess the whole thing was much too painful
for him, and he couldn't deal with any of it for very long.

Much of what I learned about the Holocaust I
probably learned in school except for when my dad would
throw in a little tidbit here and there. I was really glad and
relieved when he did start to talk about his past. After we
traveled to Germany in 1995, I finally had concrete evidence
of everything that made me proud to be his daughter.

The trip was a fabulous experience and once in a
lifetime. I was on board immediately and encouraging
everyone to go. It would have been tragic if he had not gone.
It changed my life for sure. The whole experience ran the
gamut of every possible emotion. We actually laughed quite
a bit and had several inside jokes develop during the weeks.
Here we were, a family who identified mostly with being
Irish Catholic, and we were surrounded by Jews for the first
time in our lives.

The most important part, of course, was the time we
spent at Bergen-Belsen. It was a somber time as we all just
toured the camp and listened to the Rabbi speak. Everyone
was reeling from the experience. When the clerk in the
museum gift store realized who was making purchases of
books and other souvenirs, she became very flustered and
called her supervisor over. He then said not to charge
anyone for anything, that we could have what we wanted.

feel right about charging the actual survivors of a concentration camp for any mementos. It was mind boggling.

I don't think my identity has changed much over the past twenty years as far as my heritage goes. I may be a tad bit more likely to admit my Jewish heritage and even turn my kalada Star of David jewelry to the star side. But I don't think I was ashamed of it before. I don't consider myself very religious. My three girls attend a Catholic school mostly because I consider it an academically superior school.

My dad . . . he is complicated. Any time I do try to describe him to a friend, I end up talking on and on. He was generally a good father although he made many mistakes with me especially when I was a teen. He had trouble separating and letting me grow up. I forgive him. It could have been worse. He is incredibly smart even though he doesn't appear to be. He has an excellent memory for details. He remembers things from pharmacy school that I forgot long ago. He not only learned the course material but can still remember it and use it. He has lots of common sense and a great ability to see things in a simplified version. He was always able to calm my hysteria when I was in college and on the verge of a meltdown over something ridiculous. He can put everything into perspective. He knows what the worst case scenario is because he has lived it. Everything pales in comparison to that.

I personally believe it's possible that the Holocaust had only a small role in his depressive episode. His problems stemmed from his business dealings, in my opinion. It seemed logical at the time to most that he was finally dealing with issues that had been swept under the carpet for fifty years, but I don't think that was a major factor. I'm sure it may have contributed, but in a minor way.

My family is close knit but not demonstrative in our love and respect for each other. It is just understood, a given that we like to be together and are all proud of each other. I am extremely fortunate to be in a family like this.

Joe

Childhood Dad Memories: Going to see the jazz greats with Dad – Buddy Rich, Maynard Ferguson, Count Basie, Woody Herman, we saw them all. Like when he flies, I believe Dad loses his past in jazz music. Coming home from church with Dad quiet and subdued, the curtains closed, and all of us trying to figure out what was going on. He was watching the football game and was quarter back throwing a pass into the couch but he overthrew into the window! Much silliness, funny faces, "I bet I can make you laugh," "Don't cry, I like your eyes better when they're dry. They are never really dry." Loving fresh air, the outdoors, driving, getting tan, exercising.

Since English is his second (third?) language, he talks funny. Those sprinkles that one puts on ice cream cones and cookies he called "fliddybiddies," thus prompting the question, "Can we have ice cream with fliddybiddies?" This and other words and phrases are part of our family, and my own kids even call them fliddybiddies now.

I've got the name, you know, Joseph Mueller, Unkle's name, and therefore the legacy. The legacy started early, as early as I can remember. Unkle and Tante would come over one Sunday every month for a real European-type visit – conversation, then coffee and cake at 4:00 p.m. There was always a moment when Unkle and I would be alone, in the garden, in the den, wherever, and he would ask me if I still wanted to be a doctor and tell me what a great profession and way of life it is. I was five years old telling people I wanted to be a doctor.

What evolved was the perception of pressure as I became more autonomous, and this caused huge arguments with my dad. He never really understood my perspective or what I was doing as a teenager and college student. How could he? His advice I took at the time was to study hard the first year of college so as to allow for a good start which the average student inevitably fails to do. I followed this advice, and the process became second nature. I did well and went on to med school, but was still uncertain what I really wanted to do. It seemed like much toil for an uncertain end until I discovered emergency medicine. The cowboys of medicine go into it, and I found a home. I can tell you that I love being a doctor and value tremendously the influence of Unkle and my dad. I do still think that there was huge pressure on me and that I felt I didn't need it. On the other hand, if you look at most doctors, I think you will find an abundance of early "support" which could be perceived as pressure depending on who's doing the looking.

The message I got from my dad on the Holocaust was that it is best to simply move on, to live in the present and for the future as opposed to dwelling and harping on the past, a typical American attitude. I think the best part of his story is that he has kept moving forward, moving on in a positive direction. What made him strong and a survivor was and is his ability to keep moving and see his place in the universe ultimately as an American and not a Jew or a Catholic. I think this is, in fact, the religion that suits him best.

When Dad's depression hit, I was a fourth year med student preparing to graduate (finally I was there!) and waiting to find out where my residency would be. We were also having our first baby in a matter of days, and Dad was suicidal. Mom dealt with it daily and face to face but my involvement was big. All my sisters were out of town. I had some knowledge as a med student. It became apparent to me that he was severely depressed so Mo and I went over there to his house one day. I spoke with Dad in the basement and asked him the same questions I had just learned to ask patients. We stood father and son with all the water under the bridge, and I point blank asked him eye to eye if he wanted to kill himself. He nodded affirmative. I asked how would he do it, and he looked me in the eye (looking unlike himself) and put his index finger in his mouth with his hand in the shape of a gun. I asked if he would do it any other way, and he said no. I told him to give me the gun, and he said okay. I took the gun and hid it in my apartment despite the fact that both Mo and I are afraid of guns. Then, I insisted he get treatment which he did. My mom was the rock with this, but I was intimately involved. I believe my mom helped save him by insisting that everyday he get up, get dressed, and go to work. Then, she would worry about him until he came home.

I believe the depression was a result of an acute stress piling on and overwhelming the chronic situation of the Holocaust. He dealt with that the way we all deal with problems, denial. Denial gets a bad rap, but it actually works great for a long time. However, over the years it began to fail and eventually was eroded by acute personal stress.

The trip changed his and our perspectives. It was I who made sure he went. When he told me he threw the letter in a drawer and said he wasn't going, I told him he had to. I nagged him in true Mueller fashion until he agreed. The trip allowed him to finally realize that there were others like him, that he was connected. For the family, I believe, it was our defining moment. We all exhaled and counted to ten and began talking about it. Since then, we just seem more of a family, more affectionate, closer. He is happier, more well-adjusted (what a thing for a son to say about his father).

I did steal that bottle opener in Lippstadt, by the way. The town evoked the most bitterness in me. I still feel angry toward that cute town. I realize there were bigger forces, but the loss and injustice seemed so real while visiting there. I can't say that I really want to return. But I do value my bottle opener.

I want to talk about two other people, though: Unkle and my mother.

Unkle Joseph was truly the patriarch of the family and his influence is still there. Unkle saved Dad by planting the seed that he was not Jewish. Thus, he winds up in Bergen-Belsen instead of Auschwitz. This isn't a certain ticket to survival, but Auschwitz might have meant immediate death.

Even though our family never really seemed to have a history and extended family that others had, we actually did, as I see it now. The Mueller family is actually quite involved and has a rich history with towering figures. Unkle may very well be on top of it all.

Mom has been the rock of the family and has endured, up close and personal, the full force of my dad's baggage. She has never been anything but supportive. His personality has been softened a lot by the trip, but over the last forty plus years, she has put up with a lot. In her own way, she too has a survivor mentality. In fact, she is extremely cautious, defensive, protective, and strong willed. All of us Mueller kids are defensive in our driving behaviors and lives, which one might think stems from our father's survivor syndrome. And it does. But I think our mother's influence along these lines was greater. She has instilled in all of us a tendency to be financially responsible, show up five minutes early, be aware of our environment, be prepared for the worst. Maybe this was part of the attraction between Mom and Dad? My mom is a strong, supportive, stoic woman who held together a man and his family through many years of difficult and nebulous torment.

As far as my own identity coming out of all this, I do not feel that I am Jewish. I feel connected and part of the Jewish culture, but do not buy into the religious aspect. Jews seem to believe, therefore, that I am not Jewish. Others, however, seem to feel that I am. What's a religious mosaic such as myself supposed to think?

I recall us all going to church with my mom, and Mom and Dad would fight about the fact that he wanted to stay home and listen to jazz in his underwear and smoke cigars. He would say, "Where was God when I was in the camp?"

I tried to be a good Catholic at college and even went to church every day at some point, but I never was able to keep it up. But I like being part of the Catholic world. I was raised Catholic. I went to a Catholic college by choice, Catholic med school, and married a very Irish Catholic girl. I work at a Catholic institution and find comfort in the continuity, the Jesuits, and Christian Brothers.

108

I also find warm comfort and spirituality in jazz, cigars, and hanging around the house in my underwear on Sunday morning.

My dad came to this country with nothing. Now he has a profession, a beautiful house, a forty-five year marriage to a good woman, five children – all professionals, all successfully married, no divorces – each child with three children of their own. Not bad for an orphan. My dad is an American success story.

Appendix

All pictures and document copies are from the private collection of George Levy Mueller and Family unless otherwise indicated.

Lucie Hope Levy (circa 1935)

**Georg, Max, and Lucie Levy
(before Ursula)**

**Family Portrait: Lucie, Ursula, Max, and Georg Levy
(circa 1936)**

The Levy family home in Lippstadt looking much the same today as in the 1930's. The dry goods store was on the ground floor.

Kommandantur
des Staatl. Konzentrationslagers
Sachsenhausen

Oranienburg, ben 22 XII 1938 19

Entlassungsschein

Der Jude Max L e v y   geb. am 25. 7.84

in Lippstadt

                                                          war in der Zeit
vom 12.11.38   bis 22 XII 1938   in einem Konzentrationslager untergebracht.
Die Entlassung erfolgte am:

Seine Führung war: ----

Auflage:
Sie haben sich ~~~~~~~~~~~~~~~~~~~~~~~~~~~~~
bei der Ortspolizeibehörde Ihres Wohnortes sofort
~~~~~~

zu melden.

Der Lagerkommandant:

.B.

SS-Hauptsturmführer

Kommandantur
des Staatl. Konzentrationslagers
Sachsenhausen

Oranienburg, ben 22 XII 1938 19

Entlassungsschein

Der Jude Ludwig L e v y   geb. am 7.2.82

in Lippstadt   war in der Zeit
vom 12-11.38   bis 22 XII 1938   in einem Konzentrationslager untergebracht.
Die Entlassung erfolgte am: 22 XII 1938

Seine Führung war: ----

Auflage:
Sie haben sich ~~~~~~~~~~~~~~~~~~~~~~~~~~~~~
bei der Ortspolizeibehörde Ihres Wohnortes sofort
~~~~~~

zu melden.

Der Lagerkommandant:

a.B.

SS-Hauptsturmführer

Druck: Müller, Oranienburg

Nazi records of the imprisonment and release of Max Levy and Ludwig Levy in Sachsenhausen, Germany, following Kristallnacht in November of 1938.

Ursula Levy's kindertransport name tag.

Waldman, the dog, who would ignore a piece of meat placed on his nose if told it came from Hitler.

Postcard from Lucie to George and Ursula after they were in Holland. The message says, "Dear Georg and Ursula: Thank you for your letter from you and Tante Sofie. I sent you my fountain pen so that you can, dear Georg, write to me often. Be nice to your little sister. I am happy that you soon will go to Amsterdam. That way, Tante Sofie and Onkel Albert will not have to spend money all the time for the trip to Rotterdam which does always cost something. A kiss for you nice kids and say hello to Tante Margo. Your Mommy."

Eersel. St. Jacobus Gesticht en R. K. Koloniehuis. Voorgevel.

St. Jacobus in Eersel, Holland

St. Jacobus with nuns and children playing in the yard.

St. Jacobus dining hall.

Ursula and George on steps at St. Jacobus.

Meneer v. Mackelenbergh

The day George and Ursula (standing in front) were baptized at St. Jacobus. The adults, from left to right, are Herman Weyers (acting as Godfather), Mother Renildus, Gonda Weyers (acting as Godmother), Rector Leo Weyers (who performed the baptisms), an unnamed German girl (also baptized), Mrs. v. Mackelenbergh, the brother of the German girl (also baptized), and Mr. v Mackelenbergh.

Transport list with George's name on it fifth from bottom authorizing his transport to Bergen Belsen from Westerbork. Ursula's name was on a similar list.

125

George and Ursula preparing to fly KLM to the United States.

George as an American soldier in Paris.

Survivors during the 50th Anniversary trip. George is in the upper middle part of the picture with his face in profile.

Monument at Westerbork which reads: "They gave us every burden so that we could not fulfill our destiny. Our days were over. Yes, our end had come." (Lamentations 4:18)

From left to right: Maureen, Joe, George, Katie, Jane, and Lucy at the memorial wall at Trobitz during the 50th Anniversary trip.

Dr. Thomas Rahe, curator of the museum at Bergen Belsen, with George, during the 2000 trip.

Hans Boenicke and George in Lippstadt, Germany, during the 2000 trip.

George's Aunt Irmgard and Uncle Joseph Mueller.

A recent picture of Ursula and George in Glen Ellyn.

George and Katie at the center of their five children, four sons-in-law, one daughter-in-law, and fifteen grand-children.

Made in the USA
Monee, IL
14 November 2019